THE PSYCHOLOGY OF CONSPIRACY THEORIES

Who believes in conspiracy theories, and why are some people more susceptible to them than others? What are the consequences of such beliefs? Has a conspiracy theory ever turned out to be true? *The Psychology of Conspiracy Theories* debunks the myth that conspiracy theories are a modern phenomenon, exploring their broad social contexts, from politics to the workplace. The book explains why some people are more susceptible to these beliefs than others and how they are produced by recognizable and predictable psychological processes. Updated throughout and now featuring examples from the COVID-19 pandemic and the 2021 Capitol Hill riots, this new edition of *The Psychology of Conspiracy Theories* shows us that while such beliefs are not always irrational and are not a pathological trait, they can be harmful to individuals and society.

Jan-Willem van Prooijen is Associate Professor of Social Psychology at VU Amsterdam, senior researcher at the Netherlands Institute for the Study of Crime and Law Enforcement, and Endowed Professor of Radicalization, Extremism, and Conspiracy Thinking at Maastricht University.

THE PSYCHOLOGY OF EVERYTHING

People are fascinated by psychology, and what makes humans tick. Why do we think and behave the way we do? We've all met armchair psychologists claiming to have the answers, and people that ask if psychologists can tell what they're thinking. The Psychology of Everything is a series of books which debunk the popular myths and pseudo-science surrounding some of life's biggest questions.

The series explores the hidden psychological factors that drive us, from our subconscious desires and aversions, to our natural social instincts. Absorbing, informative, and always intriguing, each book is written by an expert in the field, examining how research-based knowledge compares with popular wisdom, and showing how psychology can truly enrich our understanding of modern life.

Applying a psychological lens to an array of topics and contemporary concerns—from sex, to fashion, to conspiracy theories—The Psychology of Everything will make you look at everything in a new way.

Titles in the series:

For more information about this series, please visit: www.routledge-textbooks.com/textbooks/thepsychologyofeverything/

THE PSYCHOLOGY OF CONSPIRACY THEORIES

SECOND EDITION

JAN-WILLEM VAN PROOIJEN

Routledge
Taylor & Francis Group

LONDON AND NEW YORK

Designed cover image: Getty Images

Second edition published 2026
by Routledge
4 Park Square, Milton Park, Abingdon, Oxon, OX14 4RN

and by Routledge
605 Third Avenue, New York, NY 10158

Routledge is an imprint of the Taylor & Francis Group, an informa business

For Product Safety Concerns and Information please contact our EU representative GPSR@taylorandfrancis.com. Taylor & Francis Verlag GmbH, Kaufingerstraße 24, 80331 München, Germany.

First edition published by Routledge 2018

British Library Cataloguing-in-Publication Data
A catalogue record for this book is available from the British Library

Library of Congress Cataloging-in-Publication Data
Names: Prooijen, Jan-Willem van, 1975- author
Title: The psychology of conspiracy theories / Jan-Willem van Prooijen.
Description: Second edition. | Abingdon, Oxon; New York, NY: Routledge, 2026. | Series: Psychology of everything | Previous edition: 2018. | Includes bibliographical references. |
Identifiers: LCCN 2025030653 (print) | LCCN 2025030654 (ebook) | ISBN 9781032870571 hardback | ISBN 9781032868585 paperback | ISBN 9781003530718 ebook
Subjects: LCSH: Conspiracy theories
Classification: LCC HV6275.P756 2026 (print) | LCC HV6275 (ebook)
LC record available at https://lccn.loc.gov/2025030653
LC ebook record available at https://lccn.loc.gov/2025030654

ISBN: 9781032870571 (hbk)
ISBN: 9781032868585 (pbk)
ISBN: 9781003530718 (ebk)

DOI: 10.4324/9781003530718

Typeset in Joanna
by Deanta Global Publishing Services, Chennai, India

CONTENTS

PREFACE TO THE SECOND EDITION

When the First Edition of this book appeared in 2018, the scientific study of belief in conspiracy theories was still a relatively new and emerging research domain. The field was already in motion, however: While in the early 2000s only a few sporadic publications have appeared about the topic and conspiracy belief was not widely seen as worth studying, this was clearly changing by 2018. Scientists, policymakers, practitioners, and the general public had started to recognize the relevance of conspiracy theories to understand many of the problems society faces, including climate change, public health, immigration, societal cohesion, populism, and geopolitical conflict. Yet, no-one could have foreseen the extent to which the study of conspiracy theories would dominate scientific and public discourse in the years that followed. A huge volume of scientific publications has appeared about the topic in recent years, and most conferences within psychology and other social sciences routinely include symposia about conspiracy theories. Conspiracy theories also have had a major impact on the world in the context of impactful and recent societal events, which include the COVID-19 pandemic, electoral successes of populist movements in many countries, sustainability initiatives, and the war in Ukraine. Eventually I had to accept the inevitable: The original 2018 text has become outdated.

On average, a new edition of a book requires a change of about 30% of the original text. In this case, however, it became apparent quickly that this would not do justice to all the massive developments in science and society that were relevant for this book. While the book still has an approximately similar basic structure, and some parts of the original first text did make it into the new text, this Second Edition has revised and adjusted a large part of the original text. This is also reflected in the reference list, which contains many publications that have appeared in the past five years. Of course, there is variance across the chapters, with some chapters having retained substantial pieces of text of the First Edition, while other chapters have been rewritten almost entirely.

I had written the First Edition in a style focused on a relatively broad audience that did not require a background in psychology. In this Second Edition, I have tried to retain that style as much as possible; however, I had to balance this with the need to do justice to the vastly expanded research literature and the many developments that have taken place in this field. Furthermore, it is important to keep in mind that books within Routledge's "The Psychology of..." series have a strict upper word limit, as they need to be short and accessible introductions to a research topic. It hence was impossible to discuss all the relevant new development in the field of conspiracy theories within the space provided. As a result of these trade-offs, the Second Edition of this book may feel a bit more "academic" than the First Edition, as reflected in a higher emphasis on research findings and a lower emphasis on anecdotes and examples. Still, I have tried to keep the book accessible to any interested reader, and hope that both experts and readers with no background in psychology can appreciate this new edition.

I thank Annabelle Harris and Ceri McLardy at Routledge for encouraging me to write this Second Edition, and for their patience when the process turned out to take (much) longer than expected.

Also, my own research on conspiracy theories has expanded exponentially after the publication of the first edition in 2018. Science is teamwork, however, and I would like to thank all my collaborators and PhD students in the past years for all the work we have jointly produced on this topic—and for all the wonderful, inspirational, and also funny moments we have had while doing so. Finally, I thank my colleagues, friends, family, and of course my wife, Claudia, for their unwavering support.

Jan-Willem van Prooijen,
Amsterdam, 23 May 2025

1

THE PSYCHOLOGY OF CONSPIRACY THEORIES

About three to four decades from now, people will tell their grand-children stories of the year 2020. It was the year when the Sars-Cov-2 virus took the world by surprise. After the first cases were detected in Wuhan, China, the virus spread rapidly around the world, leaving anxiety, illness, and death in its footsteps. Most citizens have spent months in lockdown, rendering surreal footage of metropolitan cities that looked like ghost towns. The global economy largely stopped overnight, businesses went bankrupt and societal unrest soared. But the pandemic also gave rise to something else: Conspiracy theories. In the first few months of the pandemic, a common theory on social media was that the coronavirus was a bioweapon created by humans in a laboratory. Moreover, popular online conspiracy influencers promoted the theory that not a virus, but the radiation of the novel 5G mobile network was the reason why people were getting ill. This theory has inspired activist groups to arson telecommunication masts in various countries including the UK, France, and the Netherlands.

Throughout the pandemic different conspiracy theories emerged. As multiple vaccines against the coronavirus had been developed and the largest global inoculation campaign in the history of humanity began, conspiracy theories were pushed online stating

DOI: 10.4324/9781003530718-1

that Bill Gates had put microchips in the vaccines to turn people into remotely controllable robots. Other theories were less outlandish but still claimed that dangerous side-effects of the vaccines were deliberately withheld from the public for nefarious motives such as financial profit. And up until today many people are convinced that the whole COVID-19 pandemic was a hoax fabricated by powerful elites, designed to strip citizens of their basic rights. Our grandchildren will hear stories about the pandemic alright—but the content of these stories may vary widely. Some may hear how their grandparents spent their days in isolation, helped their neighbors, worked unimaginable shifts in the hospital, or found clever ways to keep their business running; but others may hear stories of how a mysterious global elite managed to deceive the world, invented a disease to oppress the people, and managed to persuade gullible citizens to inject themselves with a poisonous substance.

Whether we believe in them or not, such conspiracy theories surely are fascinating. Conspiracy theories appeal to a basic, dark fear that we all are string puppets under the control of powerful, sinister, and invisible forces. Conspiracy theories refer to hidden, secret, and malignant organizations that influence our lives without us being aware of it. Many conspiracy theories elicit a sense of "What if?" among people: Can these theories be true, and what would that imply for how we live our lives? Do we really understand the way that the world operates, or have we been deceived all along? There is something irresistibly mysterious, intriguing, but also frightening to a credible conspiracy theory, and therefore conspiracy theories have the potential to capture the attention of a broad audience.

Such widespread appeal can for instance be seen in the prominent place that conspiracy theories have in popular culture. Many well-known blockbuster movies and series are based on the central idea of people being deceived or threatened by a conspiracy of evil and hidden forces. At the time of writing this, one of the most popular Netflix series is "Stranger Things", which describes how a group of adolescents in a small US town gets confronted with peculiar and dangerous creatures from an alternative dimension. This dimension was opened through secret experiments by a mysterious government program that has little interest in the well-being of local citizens. The conspiracy relentlessly continuous to pursue its hidden goals even when it becomes apparent that opening this alternative dimension poses a threat to the entire world. Another example is "The Matrix"—a movie in which viewers are led to believe that life as we know it is a Virtual Reality illusion that has been deliberately pulled over our eyes. Human beings actually are prisoners of a conspiracy of hostile and highly intelligent computers, who utilize our life energy as efficient batteries. Mysterious conspiracies that are purely evil, operate largely in the shadows, and seem to stop at nothing to achieve their wicked goals clearly appeal to people's imagination.

These issues reflect a basic truth about conspiracy theories: While not everyone may be ready to admit it, many people find conspiracy theories entertaining. Together with a group of students we conducted a range of experiments that exposed research participants to well-known conspiracy theories. In one study, participants read how a powerful conspiracy had ignited the 2019 Notre Dame fire in Paris deliberately; in another study, participants read how the infamous sex offender Jeffrey Epstein did not commit suicide but was murdered in his prison cell. Our results indicated that people found such conspiratorial narratives more entertaining (e.g., more mysterious, exciting, attention-grabbing, less boring) than the official explanation of these events. Moreover, we found that people who believe conspiracy theories tend to have stronger sensation-seeking tendencies—a desire for new, intense, and varied experiences, and a willingness to take risks for the sake of these experiences (Van Prooijen et al., 2022). Spending hours learning about a new conspiracy theory is a perfect recipe against boredom.

One factor that contributes to the widespread appeal of conspiracy theories is the possibility that they might be true—and in fact, conspiracies sometimes can and do occur. In fact, the Holocaust was the result of a real conspiracy. Whilst Jewish people were already widely persecuted and killed in Nazi-Germany in the 1930s and early 1940s, initially the Nazis had hoped that due to the hostile climate most Jews would leave the country voluntarily. This did not happen on the scale desired by Hitler, however, and in January 1942 a conspiracy of 15 high-ranked Nazis and SS-officers secretly gathered in a villa at Wannsee near Berlin. Although Hitler did not attend in person, the meeting had the purpose of designing a concrete plan to carry out Hitler's recent orders—which boiled down to "physically exterminating" all the Jews in Europe. This meeting, commonly known as the "Wannsee conference", marked the beginning of the mass deportation of Jewish people to Nazi death camps, where they were murdered in gas chambers on an unprecedented scale. The Holocaust is now recognized as one of the biggest tragedies in human history. Yet, it was not until 1947 that a legal prosecutor found evidence that the Wannsee conference took place, by discovering the strictly classified minutes of this secret meeting.

This book is about the psychology of conspiracy theories. Many different conspiracy theories circle the Internet and social media, some of them plausible or at least theoretically possible (e.g., perhaps secret service agencies sometimes do push the limits of what is legally or morally acceptable), others are rather outlandish and highly unlikely (e.g., I strongly doubt that the Earth is ruled by a race of alien lizards disguised as humans). Furthermore, there are many examples of actual conspiracy formation throughout history—ranging from modern times (e.g., the FIFA corruption scandal; the Volkswagen Diesel scandal) to for instance the Roman Senate conspiracy that killed Julius Caesar—and hence, not all conspiracy theories are necessarily irrational.

Moreover, different conspiracy theories have different effects on people. People who believed that COVID-19 was created in the laboratory were more likely to prepare themselves for mayhem (e.g., hoarding everyday goods) while people who believed that COVID-19 was a hoax were less likely to display containment-related behavior (e.g., physical distancing) (Imhoff & Lamberty, 2020). Likewise, the same conspiracy theory may have different effects on people depending on their social or cultural background. Exposing US citizens to the theory that the US government had shady deals with pharmaceutical companies during the pandemic made them perceive the US societal system as less fair; but exposing Chinese citizens to the same conspiracy theory (about the US government) made them perceive the Chinese societal system as fairer (Mao et al., 2024). Despite all these complexities, in the present book I will argue that people's tendency to believe in conspiracy theories is rooted in similar, recognizable, and predictable psychological processes.

WHAT IS A CONSPIRACY THEORY?

A common and simple definition of a conspiracy theory is the belief that a number of actors join together in secret agreement, in order to achieve a hidden goal which is perceived to be unlawful or malevolent. This is a broad definition, and accordingly, conspiracy theories can take many forms and emerge in many different spheres of life. People can hold conspiracy theories about the government, or governmental institutions (e.g., secret service agencies). People can hold conspiracy theories about entire branches of industry (e.g., the pharmaceutical industry; oil companies) or about scientific research (e.g., climate change conspiracy theories). At the far-right, conspiracy theories about ethnic minorities are common, a case in point being the Great Replacement Theory (which states that a conspiracy exists to gradually replace the White population of Western nations with immigrants and Muslims). Employees on the work floor also often hold conspiracy beliefs about their management, such as beliefs that managers have a hidden agenda to pursue selfish goals. Conspiracy theories may occur in sports (e.g., beliefs that the referee was bribed by the opposing team). Also in their personal life, people may hold conspiracy theories by thinking that others conspire against them personally—although the latter, more personally oriented forms of conspiracy theories are more commonly regarded as examples of interpersonal paranoia, which is qualitatively different from conspiracy beliefs that make assumptions of how large groups of citizens are being deceived by formal authorities.

Various attempts have been made to specify conspiracy theories further. One publication stated that conspiracy theories have several more specific dimensions (Douglas & Sutton, 2023). Notably, these authors claim that conspiracy theories (a) oppose publicly accepted understandings of events ("oppositional"), (b) describe malevolent or forbidden acts, (c) ascribe agency to individuals and groups, (d) are more often false than other types of beliefs ("epistemically risky") and (e) are social constructs that provide a basis for an alternative shared reality. Admittedly, I find these five dimensions unsatisfactory. While I can agree with three of them (specifically b, c, and e), admittedly I am quite critical of two others—specifically, the notions that conspiracy theories are by definition "epistemically risky" and "oppositional".

These two dimensions clearly confuse "correlated" with "defining" features. A correlated feature means that a variable often, but not always co-occurs with the phenomenon of interest; for a dimension to be "defining", however, it needs to be inherent to the phenomenon. Put differently: Many conspiracy theories may be epistemically risky and oppositional (as said, I am not disputing these are likely correlated features). But if we can easily identify conspiracy theories that are not epistemically risky or oppositional, it means these are not defining features. As to epistemically risky, this is often but not necessarily true. Sometimes people have good reason to suspect a conspiracy, and some conspiracy theories can be quite plausible—in fact, corruption is a major problem in many countries. But without conclusive evidence such suspicions still are a conspiracy theory. Hence, "epistemically risky" is not a defining property of a conspiracy theory. Also, the assumption that conspiracy theories would necessarily be "oppositional" is a mistake. While many conspiracy theories are oppositional, it is quite easy to identify conspiracy theories that are not.

Because, what "public understandings" do conspiracy theories oppose exactly? In the 1980s, almost 80% of the US population believed that a conspiracy killed John F. Kennedy (more recent polls still indicated about 60%). When the Bush administration in 2003 stated that Saddam Hussain was hiding weapons of mass destruction, this was not oppositional—it was a formal US government position, informed by legitimate security agencies; most US citizens believed it, and many other national governments in the UN believed it too. What is "oppositional" further depends on time and culture. Putin's 2022 rhetoric assuming that nefarious conspiracies of the Ukrainian government and NATO attempted to harm Russian interests may be oppositional to citizens of Western nations; but for a Russian citizen living in Moscow, it would be quite oppositional to think (let alone publicly proclaim) otherwise. In Nazi-Germany during the late 1930s, it was mainstream (not oppositional) to believe in Jewish conspiracies for world domination. And in Medieval times, there was widespread agreement about the existence of witches that conspired with the devil to cause death and misery in human societies. These beliefs may be oppositional now, but they were not back then. And yet, all these beliefs are, were, and always have been, conspiracy theories.

Instead, I propose that any belief needs to possess the following five critical ingredients to qualify as a conspiracy theory. Here they are:

1. *Patterns* – Any conspiracy theory explains events by establishing nonrandom connections between actions, objects, and people. Put differently, a conspiracy theory assumes that the chain of incidents that caused a suspect event did not occur through coincidence.
2. *Agency* – A conspiracy theory assumes that a suspect event was caused on purpose by deliberate actors. There was a sophisticated

and detailed plan, which was intentionally developed and carried out.

3. *Coalitions* – A conspiracy theory always involves a coalition or group of multiple actors (often, but not necessarily humans—people may also form conspiracy theories about aliens, supernatural beings, or sentient technology such as AI-agents). If one believes that a single individual, a lone wolf, is responsible for a suspect event, this belief is not a conspiracy theory—for the simple reason that it does not involve a conspiracy.

4. *Hostility* – A conspiracy theory tends to assume the suspected coalition to pursue goals that are evil, selfish, or otherwise not in the public interest. People may sometimes suspect a benevolent conspiracy, and benevolent conspiracies indeed do exist (as adults we conspire every year to convince children of the existence of Santa Claus). But the term "conspiracy theory" as we study it in scientific research is exclusive to conspiracies that are suspected to be hostile.

5. *Secrecy* – Conspiracy theories are about coalitions that operate in secret. A conspiracy that is exposed and hence proven true (e.g., the Wannsee conference) is no longer a "theory"; instead, it is an established example of an actual conspiracy. Conspiracy theories are thus by definition unproven.

But even when taking these dimensions into account, different types of conspiracy beliefs exist. The most common distinction is between specific conspiracy theories and generalized conspiracy mentality. Specific conspiracy theories refer to concrete theories about specific events, such as theories that the NASA faked the moon landings, that 9/11 was an inside job by the US government, or that the COVID-19 pandemic was a hoax. Generalized conspiracy mentality, however, refers to a general belief that many events in the world were caused by conspiracies. Such specific and generalized conspiracy beliefs often are highly correlated, but there are also differences. For example, generalized conspiracy mentality is less malleable across situations and over time than specific beliefs (Imhoff et al., 2022). In a longitudinal study with five waves during the 2020 US presidential elections, specific conspiracy beliefs about election fraud turned out to be highly sensitive to the events that transpired. Generalized conspiracy mentality turned out to be rather stable over time among participants, however (Wang & Van Prooijen, 2023).

THE PSYCHOLOGY OF CONSPIRACY THEORIES

"Have you ever considered the possibility that our theories might be true?" This is a question that I regularly get through email from Dutch citizens who are active on conspiracy websites. Often these messages have an angry tone, voiced by citizens who somehow feel offended by my research on conspiracy theories, and who seem keen on persuading me that the COVID-19 pandemic really was a hoax, or that vaccines truly are poisonous. These messages typically (and wrongly) assume that if one studies the psychology of conspiracy theories, one necessarily proposes that all the conspiracy theories that people believe are invalid, or that people who believe in conspiracy theories are pathological.

In fact, the definition of a conspiracy theory does not assume them to be false per se, it assumes them to be unproven (secrecy). Accordingly, the psychology of conspiracy theories is not about the question which conspiracy theories are true or false—it is about the question who does or does not believe in them. There are many conspiracy theories that can be considered irrational in the face of logic or scientific evidence, and the fact that many people nevertheless believe in them is good reason to study this topic. Furthermore, I am willing to submit here that I am highly skeptical of some of the rather grandiose conspiracy theories that circle the Internet. I find it highly implausible that COVID-19 was created in the lab, or that 5G radiation makes people ill. Humans certainly have been on the moon. And the 9/11 terrorist strikes were carried out by a group of 19 Al Qaeda suicide terrorists—which is not a conspiracy theory by the above definition, because the evidence to support this claim is so overwhelming that it is safe to say that the conspiracy of these 19 terrorists has been exposed (i.e., there is no "secrecy" anymore). But what I think about these specific conspiracy theories is not the focus of this book.

This book focuses on the *psychology* of conspiracy theories, which is the scientific study of why some people are more likely than others to believe in conspiracy theories. Typical questions that are part of the psychology of conspiracy theories are: What personality factors predict whether someone believes or disbelieves conspiracy theories? To what extent does belief in one conspiracy theory (e.g., about the pharmaceutical industry) predict the likelihood of believing in a different conspiracy theory (e.g., JFK)? In what situations are people more, and in what situations are people less likely to believe in conspiracy theories? And what are the consequences of conspiracy theories for believers' feelings and behaviors? To study these issues, one does not need the conspiracy theory that is under investigation to be necessarily false, nor does newly emerging evidence that an actual conspiracy occurred compromise any of the conclusions that are drawn in this research area.

Let me briefly illuminate this principle by drawing a comparison with the psychology of religion. Many social scientists study religious beliefs, and one typical finding in this research domain is that religious people cling more strongly to their faith in unpredictable, frightening situations (I'm sure many readers recognize the desire to say a little prayer when they are scared). The theory behind this finding is that people have a need to feel that they are to some extent in control of their environment. Unpredictable situations make people feel less in control, and therefore, people start relying more strongly on external sources of control—such as God (Kay et al., 2010). Is it necessary for this line of research to also prove or disprove—or at least make assumptions of—the actual existence of God? My answer would be a succinct "No": The mere observation that people differ strongly in their religiousness is sufficient to raise the legitimate question why some people do, and others do not, entertain certain religious beliefs. The finding that people are more religious in frightening situations teaches us something about the psychological processes underlying religion: For instance, one possible interpretation of these research findings is that belief in God can be a source of comfort in scary situations. This conclusion does not make any judgment of the question whether God exists or not, nor does it imply a value judgment for believers or nonbelievers.

The principle for the psychology of conspiracy theories is the same: It is perfectly possible to study these beliefs without knowing for sure whether certain specific conspiracy theories are true or false. In fact, I know of one published research study that examined belief in a conspiracy theory that later did turn out to be true. The study focused specifically on the Watergate affair. In 1972, a group of five men were caught burglarizing the Democratic National Committee headquarters in the Watergate hotel, Washington DC. The burglary was part of a bigger scheme that involved influential Republicans spying on the Democratic Party for political gain, which included bugging the offices of Democratic opponents, and other abuses of power. Many high-ranked White House officials, including President Nixon himself, initially denied any involvement after the burglars were caught. In the investigation that followed, however, the evidence increasingly suggested that Nixon actively tried to cover up his personal involvement in the burglary and other illegal activities associated with it. Eventually, the public release of tape recordings that Nixon had of meetings held in his office supported his role in a cover-up, leading him to resign his presidency on August 9, 1974.

Two academic researchers, Thomas Wright and Jack Arbuthnot, conducted a study on how suspicious people were of the Watergate affair as it unfolded (Wright & Arbuthnot, 1974). The study was conducted in May 1973—which was before the Senate hearings had taken place, before the Supreme Court had ordered Nixon's tape recordings to be made public, and hence before the personal involvement of Nixon in the Watergate affair was proven beyond reasonable doubt. At that point in time, the allegation that President Nixon himself was an active player in the Watergate scandal was still a "conspiracy theory" according to the definition presented earlier. In their study, the researchers were particularly interested in the factors that would predict how suspicious people are of the possible role that Nixon might have played during Watergate. They tested if people who have a structural tendency to distrust others would be more suspicious of Nixon's involvement. They also examined the role of political ideology and tested whether Democrats or Republicans would be more suspicious of Nixon. The results indicated that the stronger people distrust others in their daily life, the more likely they were to perceive a conspiracy involving Nixon. Relatedly, Democrats were more likely than Republicans to believe this conspiracy theory.

What followed is well known: Yes, it was true. Nixon actively tried to cover up his role in Watergate and was personally involved in the illegal extraction of sensitive information about his political opponents, which he used to his political advantage. Nixon's personal involvement in the Watergate scandal no longer classifies as a "conspiracy theory" given that there is no secrecy anymore: The conspiracy has been exposed, it is therefore no longer a "theory", and Watergate has become a textbook example of an actual conspiracy that took place at the highest political level. Should we now abandon Wright and Arbuthnot's conclusions? Does the fact that this conspiracy theory turned out true compromise their results in any way?

I do not think so. Whilst few people dispute the role of Nixon in Watergate nowadays, back in May 1973 this issue was still unproven and subject to intense public debate. The research question of Wright and Arbuthnot was not whether this conspiracy theory was true or false; the question was what factors would predict citizens' belief in them at a point in time when the evidence for this theory was still inconclusive. The results that they observed have been replicated by multiple researchers, and in the context of many other conspiracy theories. People who are inclined to distrust other people are more likely to believe in conspiracy theories than people who are inclined to trust other people. Furthermore, people particularly believe in conspiracy theories about groups that are ideologically dissimilar. Democrats therefore are more likely to believe theories that involve a Republican conspiracy, and Republicans are more likely to believe theories that involve a Democrat conspiracy. These were the conclusions that followed from Wright and Arbuthnot's study, and these conclusions still hold today.

The psychology of conspiracy theories examines who believes or disbelieves these theories instead of whether a certain conspiracy theory is true or false. I have no more knowledge about the likelihood of certain conspiracy theories than other citizens, nor do I have access to classified government intelligence—and this is not necessary to study the psychology of conspiracy theories. In the chapters that follow, I will highlight what makes people susceptible to conspiracy theories. In the remainder of this chapter, however, I will deal with two lingering issues regarding the psychology of conspiracy theories: Should we care about whether people hold such beliefs, and should we pathologize people who believe in conspiracy theories—including the relatively absurd ones?

SHOULD WE CARE ABOUT CONSPIRACY THEORIES?

Psychology offers a scientific approach that helps to establish what personality or situational factors predict belief or disbelief in conspiracy theories. After having established that this approach implies that we are not trying to prove or disprove a particular conspiracy theory, an important question becomes whether we should care about conspiracy beliefs at all. If some conspiracy theories can be true, is it not desirable that groups of citizens investigate them? Should we consider conspiracy theories as a form of harmless entertainment? Or can conspiracy theories be detrimental to people's lives and to society at large, and should we be concerned about those beliefs?

My argument is the latter: We should be concerned, because in many cases conspiracy theories are irrational, yet they can do real harm to real people. Let me first establish that I am not saying that we should follow the leaders of our society—politicians, managers, powerful media figures—without any criticism or scrutiny. A healthy critical mindset implies that we should carefully evaluate the actions of those in power, and express concern if we see bad policy or suspect malpractice. Admittedly, sometimes there can be a thin line between healthy skepticism versus destructive conspiracy theorizing. But a critical mindset does not mean uncritically accepting any bizarre or far-fetched conspiracy theory. Indeed, believing conspiracy theories is generally associated with a relatively uncritical mindset (Van Prooijen, 2019).

While one can surely find examples of actual conspiracy formation, the truth is that the vast majority of conspiracy theories that citizens have endorsed throughout the ages turned out to be false (Pipes, 1997). Moreover, notorious conspiracy theorists are actually quite bad at uncovering truly existing corruption or other conspiracies (Lewandowsky et al., 2020). My concern is particularly targeted at the many conspiracy theories that defy logic, ignore scientific evidence, or place blame on innocent people or groups—and in many ways belief in such conspiracy theories can be damaging. What people believe drives their behavior; and the more irrational these beliefs are, the more irrational the behavior it produces.

The Internet is filled with misinformation and conspiracy theories about vaccines, making people reluctant to get themselves or their children vaccinated. During the COVID-19 pandemic the anti-vaccination movement gained momentum, for an important part due to conspiracy theories portraying the mRNA vaccines as dangerous. Such conspiracy theories can lower vaccination intentions directly (Loomba et al., 2021) or indirectly by helping people justify their existing hesitancy to get vaccinated (Van Prooijen & Böhm, 2024). Conspiracy theories also reduce parent's willingness to inoculate their children with childhood vaccines. Accordingly, in recent years lower vaccination rates in many communities have increased the prevalence of diseases such as measles and whooping cough. One pertinent idea within the anti-vaccination movement is that childhood vaccines cause autism, and that the pharmaceutical industry conspires to keep the evidence for this a secret. As a result, many people avoid vaccines, putting themselves, their children, and others at unnecessary risk for dangerous and avoidable illnesses. Scientific evidence shows no relationship between vaccines and autism. Any responsible parent should make sure that their children get the appropriate vaccines at the right time. It is belief in conspiracy theories that make many parents decide otherwise.

Conspiracy beliefs also influence voting behavior and can therefore determine the outcomes of elections that shape society. In Chapter 5 I will illuminate that belief in conspiracy theories is associated with a preference for relatively populist or extreme political currents: Radical socialist parties at the left end of the political spectrum, and particularly anti-immigration populist parties at the right end of the political spectrum. Also, conspiracy theories are associated with a rejection of a system of representative democracy and makes people more open to an autocratic system where a strong leader has excessive power. Relatedly, conspiracy theories can inspire and legitimize radical political action. Many people who stormed Capitol Hill on 6 January 2021 did so because of the conspiracy theory that the presidential elections had been stolen by Democrats to favor Joe Biden. Conspiracy theories often portray political opponents as enemies, and this can prompt the belief that silencing or harming these opponents is morally righteous or necessary.

Conspiracy theories are not a harmless pastime. A recent review of the literature has suggested that conspiracy theories can harm the three dimensions of sustainability, either directly by decreasing sustainable attitudes and behaviors, or indirectly by legitimizing existing unsustainable attitudes and behaviors. More specifically, widespread conspiracy theories can be detrimental to social sustainability by damaging public health and well-being, fracturing social cohesion, and deteriorating basic human rights such as safety and democracy; they can harm environmental sustainability through decreased support for reducing carbon emissions, investing in clean energy sources, and protecting fragile ecosystems; and, conspiracy theories can hurt economic sustainability by reducing public trust and cooperation, by decreasing support for sustainable technological innovation, and by harming the international relationships necessary for fair trade (Van Prooijen et al., 2025). There can be beneficial effects of conspiracy theories as well, sometimes: Conspiracy theories can improve transparency of leaders and open a debate within society about important topics. But most of the direct or indirect effects of conspiracy theories are harmful, for believers, their social environment, and society. This suggests good reason to study these beliefs: Understanding the psychological roots of belief in implausible conspiracy theories might ultimately help in finding interventions that may reduce people's willingness to believe or spread them.

IS BELIEF IN CONSPIRACY THEORIES PATHOLOGICAL?

Passenger airplane engines often leave a condensation trail. These cloud-like trails in the sky are caused by water particles in the exhaust gasses, which are quickly transformed into ice crystals due to low temperatures at high altitudes. But so-called "Chemtrail" conspiracy theories assume an evil scheme behind these condensation trails. According to Chemtrail conspiracy theories, airplane condensation trails are actually chemical or biological substances released in the air on purpose by an evil conspiracy—usually the government. Multiple variants of these chemtrail conspiracy theories exist. A common one is that the government tries to influence the weather with these chemicals. Another variant of the theory is that these chemicals are a form of mind-control. For instance, they are designed to keep the population meek and docile, thereby allowing the government to carry out their evil plans without having to fear for a revolution by a righteously outraged crowd.

It is safe to say that this conspiracy theory is irrational. If passenger planes would indeed be equipped with technology to spray chemicals, airline technicians doing a routine check-up on a plane would easily discover this. Furthermore, scientific measurements would quickly detect the presence of strange, unknown, or harmful chemicals in the atmosphere, and would also be able to track down where these chemicals come from. None of this has happened, and most scientists, journalists, and the Environmental Protection Agency (EPA) agree that Chemtrails do not exist (readers who distrust these official sources might be interested in the fact that also the whistleblower Edward Snowden, who had access to the darkest secrets of US intelligence agencies, has confirmed that neither aliens nor chemtrails exist). Should we consider belief in this irrational conspiracy theory as pathological? It might be tempting to dismiss chemtrail believers as mentally ill. But the evidence suggests otherwise. Let me put it this way: If belief in such a relatively absurd conspiracy theory indicates pathology, we would live in a highly pathological society. In a 2017 sample that was representative for the US population, about 10% believed some form of the chemtrail conspiracy theory to be "completely" true, and another 29% rated the theory as "somewhat true". Moreover, about 61% of online discourse about geoengineering was not about science but about chemtrails (Tingley & Wagner, 2017). In a 2019 Statista poll of the US population, about 8% of the sample strongly believed in chemtrails, and another 11% somewhat believed this conspiracy theory.[1]

If already a sizeable number of people believe a relatively absurd theory like Chemtrails, how common then are more mainstream conspiracy theories, such as about the pharmaceutical industry, or the origins of the coronavirus? In a nationally representative sample of the US adult population, citizens were asked to indicate their agreement with the following statement: "The Food and Drug Administration is deliberately preventing the public from getting natural cures for cancer and other diseases because of pressure from drug companies". This is a statement that we cannot exclude with the same level of confidence as Chemtrails, but still, it does assume an exceptionally evil mindset among a large number of medical professionals (including thousands of independent scientists and medical specialists around the world who know a few things about the actual effectiveness of these natural cures and are free to speak up). How many people believed this statement? As it turned out, 37% agreed to this statement, and yet another 31% was unsure ("neither agree nor disagree"). Only 32% of the sample disagreed (Oliver & Wood, 2014). As to the COVID-19 pandemic, a YouGov poll conducted in March 2023 showed that 31% of the US population believed that the theory, that the virus responsible for COVID-19 originated from a Chinese laboratory, was "definitely true"; another 35% rated this theory as "probably true". On the question whether the virus was released on purpose, 18% rated this as "definitely true", and another 28% as "probably true".[2]

Conspiracy theories are far too widespread to dismiss belief in them as pathological. They are a common part of people's understanding of the world, just as various other forms of belief are. Many citizens believe that it is possible to predict the future from the lines in one's hand, or that the success of a newly formed romantic relationship depends on how well the zodiac signs of the two partners match. While these new-age ideas are highly implausible in light of scientific evidence as well, belief in these ideas also is not considered pathological. Normal citizens, in all branches of society, endorse a variety of implausible beliefs, which includes conspiracy theories. Although various mental illnesses certainly can exacerbate conspiracy thinking, the psychology of conspiracy theories is primarily the domain of social psychology: The study of how ordinary citizens think, feel, and act in their everyday life.

NOTES

1 https://www.statista.com/statistics/959559/conspiracy-belief-government-control-population-chemtrails/
2 https://today.yougov.com/politics/articles/45389-americans-believe-covid-origin-lab

2

EXISTENTIAL THREATS AND CONSPIRACY THEORIES

"How do you explain the fact that conspiracy theories are on the rise?" This is a question that I get exceptionally often—from students, from members of an audience after giving a talk, or from journalists who are writing a newspaper article on conspiracy theories. But that "fact" is ambiguous at best, and the question lacks specificity. Whether conspiracy theories—or anything else for that matter—are "on the rise" depends on what previous era one wishes to compare them with. Altogether, it is not so clear to me that conspiracy theories would be "on the rise". Longitudinal studies find no evidence for an increase in conspiracy beliefs over the past few decades (Uscinski et al., 2022). They do spread easily in the online environment, however (Vosoughi et al., 2018), and their visibility and impact might have increased, as for instance reflected in decreasing vaccination rates and increased support for populist movements. I am certainly open to the possibility that in recent years—also in light of a pandemic stimulating many conspiracy theories, wars in Ukraine and Gaza, and increased support for populist movements around the world—conspiracy theories have had more impact now than about 20 years ago. But in the long run, I dispute the assertion that there is a stable trend towards an increased number of people believing in conspiracy theories. Are people nowadays truly more

DOI: 10.4324/9781003530718-2

likely to believe conspiracy theories than, say, 200 years ago? That is quite debatable.

An alternative way to interpret current events is that due to a variety of factors conspiracy theories could be making a comeback in terms of the public attention they receive and the impact they have on for instance health and polarization; but that does not mean more people than ever before believe them. In his 2020 book "The Nature of Conspiracy Theories", Michael Butter makes the case that conspiracy beliefs have mostly gone down since the 1950s (Butter, 2020)—which strikes me as a reasonable assumption. For example, antisemitic conspiracy theories (such as the beliefs in Jewish conspiracies for world domination) were widely polarizing the population against Jewish people across Europe in the 1930s, and the consequences are well-known. In the United States, two political scientists from the university of Miami (helped by a team of trained research assistants) analyzed published letters that US citizens had sent to the Chicago Tribune and the New York Times (Uscinski & Parent, 2014). The letters spanned a time period of 120 years, ranging from 1890 to 2010. Each year was about equally represented in the sample of letters, and the letters to be analyzed were randomly selected out of all the letters that were published during this period. Of primary interest to the researchers was the extent to which these letters contained conspiracy theories. In the end, these researchers read, and coded for conspiratorial content, a total of 104,803 published letters.

As might be expected, there is variation across the years in the extent to which the letters contain conspiratorial content. Furthermore, in different time periods people wrote about different conspiracy theories. But over time, there was no trend upwards in the proportion of letters that contained conspiracy theories. In fact, there were two time periods that seemed to stand out in frequency of conspiratorial content, but both were not in the new millennium. The first time period when there was evidence for increased conspiratorial content was around the year 1900, during the peak of the

Second Industrial Revolution. The second time period when there was evidence for increased conspiratorial content was in the late 1940s–early 1950s: At the start of the Cold War. These data underscore that also at other times in the past century conspiracy theories have been quite popular.

Of course, the study with the letters ended in 2010, and a lot has happened since. Conspiracy theories are everywhere on the Internet and social media. They proliferate in online communities that serve as conspiratorial "echo-chambers". As a result, conspiratorial movements have emerged that for instance believe in a "Deep State" of societal elites pulling the strings (e.g., QAnon), that dispute the reality of climate change, or that actively rally against vaccines. It is clear that the online world has substantial implications for conspiracy beliefs. Conspiracy theories can be disseminated faster than ever before—if disaster strikes in New York, people in Sydney can read conspiracy theories about the event in less than an hour on X, Facebook, or Instagram. Moreover, popular conspiracy influencers (e.g., Alex Jones) that would struggle to get a podium in the regular media, can reach millions of people through their own YouTube channels (and earn a fortune in the process). And as the Internet provides a lot of contradictory information—providing a platform for both valid, scientifically grounded information and misinformation—it is increasingly difficult for citizens to figure out what is true or false.

At the same time, it would be a mistake to blame the human tendency to believe conspiracy theories on the online environment only. Conspiracy theories have flourished throughout human history, well before the existence of Internet and social media. The extent to which people endorse conspiracy theories fluctuates over time, and technological developments may contribute to that. But in their basis, conspiracy theories are rooted in a subjective, psychological state that is inherent to the human condition. They are a natural reaction to threatening social situations that elicit aversive feelings, including fear, loss of control, and uncertainty. The more strongly people experience such aversive emotions, the more likely it is that they assign blame for distressing events to different groups. As a consequence, conspiracy theories can be expected particularly in the wake of negative emotions, aversive life circumstances, rapid societal changes, or distressing societal events.

An appropriate way to put it is that novel technology may trigger people's basic, inborn predispositions, which in turn produces the psychological outcomes associated with those predispositions. For example, fear-mongering, alarmist messages about societal events are relatively likely to go viral on social media (Milli et al., 2023). People are more willing to read and repost such messages, and algorithms sometimes prioritize such messages in the newsfeed of online users. The aversive emotions that these messages arouse, in turn, increases people's belief in conspiracy theories. In this example, the dynamics of the online environment may trigger conspiracy theories; but it does so only by capitalizing on basic, ancient psychological mechanisms of how people regulate their negative emotions. The reason why such fear-arousing messages may have these effects is because of a basic psychological relationship between existential threats and belief in conspiracy theories.

CONSPIRACY THEORIES AND EXISTENTIAL THREATS

People regularly are confronted with societal crisis situations—rapid changes in society that could potentially threaten their wellbeing, their way of life, or even their existence. Examples of such crisis situations are terrorist attacks, natural disasters, wars, revolutions, economic and financial crises, disease epidemics, and the like. Such existentially threatening situations almost invariably lead to conspiracy theories. Two key examples of sudden, unexpected crises in modern history that inspired widespread conspiracy theories are the 9/11 terrorist strikes and the assassination of John F. Kennedy. Both were events that shocked society, that installed strong feelings of fear and uncertainty in people, and that gave people the feeling that the world would never be the same again. Many people have "flashbulb memories" about these events as they still vividly recall what they were doing when they first heard the news. Both events also initiated conspiracy theories that are still being endorsed today by large groups of citizens, and that many people by now have internalized as historical "facts".

But we do not need to restrict ourselves to the past century to find a connection between existential threats and conspiracy theories. In Medieval Times there are examples abound of crisis situations that initiated widespread belief in conspiracy theories. Medical science was not as advanced as our current generation is used to, and it was common for young children to die of a range of dangerous diseases that nowadays are easily prevented with vaccines. Furthermore, there was no understanding of viruses or bacteria (or the importance of personal hygiene for that matter), and antibiotics were yet to be discovered. As a consequence, disease epidemics were frequent and would kill many people, but people were unable to fully understand how these diseases originated. People therefore often blamed these epidemics on people or groups in society, and such scapegoating regularly took the form of conspiracy theories. For instance, the Jewish community was a frequent target of conspiracy theories suggesting that they had a causal role in crisis situations such as disease epidemics or setbacks during the crusades, stimulating widespread persecution of Jewish communities in Medieval Europe (Pipes, 1997).

These are just examples of a more general principle, stipulated by the Existential Threat Model of Conspiracy Theories: In challenging, threatening times that elicit aversive feelings and emotions among large groups of people, conspiracy theories flourish (Van Prooijen, 2020). People blame people or groups that they felt uncomfortable about to begin with and come up with theories that explain the harm they experience through a malevolent conspiracy. As a result, conspiracy theories will increase in the population once there is widespread concern about a high-profile terrorist attack, a natural disaster, an economic or financial crisis, a war, a revolution, and so on. Furthermore, conspiracy theories are more likely among people who structurally live in distressing circumstances (e.g., poverty) or have personality traits that predispose them to feel threatened easily. Also, events that pose no direct threat to peoples' own lives or well-being can stimulate conspiracy theories, if it captures the attention of a large audience. For example, the unexpected death of a celebrity may cause feelings of distress among many citizens (although particularly in such cases also other motives to believe in conspiracy theories are likely to play a role, including a desire for entertainment).

Even imaginary crisis situations can cause conspiracy beliefs. A case in point is the conspiracy theory that the 1969 Apollo moon landings were filmed in a TV studio. One might reason that these conspiracy theories were not a reaction to an "objective" crisis situation—it was a reaction to a positive event where humanity and science reached a new level of accomplishment. But someone who believes that the government continuously and willfully deceives the nation subjectively experiences the nation as being in crisis. Many people hold general conspiratorial beliefs about the government, and these beliefs are distressing in and of themselves, which causes further conspiracy theorizing. This is a well-known insight in the psychology of conspiracy theories: Belief in one conspiracy theory stimulates belief in other conspiracy theories. In this case, citizens who hold conspiracy theories about the government are likely to approach any action of that government—including a monument of scientific accomplishment like the moon landings—with skepticism, and with additional conspiracy theories.

THE ROLE OF DISTRESS

To understand why experiencing existential threats increases belief in conspiracy theories, we need to establish how people cope when they feel distressed. The most common response to threatening events is to become vigilant: People start paying close attention to their environment, ruminate, and try to establish the causes of their negative feelings. Fear, loss of control, uncertainty, and other distressed feelings thus lead people to try and make sense of their physical and social environment. Such increased sense-making is an automatic response that likely is rooted in an instinct for self-preservation. Distressed feelings signal that there are imminent threats in the environment. Paying close attention to this environment therefore increases the chances of the organism to effectively cope with these threats and survive.

As part of this self-preservation instinct, evolutionary psychologists have noted that people tend to be risk-averse in the face of uncertain and possibly threatening situations. This is captured in Error Management Theory which forms an evolutionary framework to understand many of the biases that people have, and the mistakes that they make, in everyday life (Haselton & Buss, 2000). This theory states that when the costs of various possible mistakes structurally differ, people will evolve to make the less costly mistake. Imagine seeing a long object in the grass, and it is unclear whether the object is a stick or a snake. In such cases, it is a natural response for people to be cautious and assume the object to be a snake. Mistakes do not have equal consequences in this situation: Someone who picks up the object assuming it to be a stick may die if it turns out to be a venomous snake. But for someone who assumes the object to be a snake and hence acts cautiously, it does not matter whether that judgment is correct or not. If one is mistaken and the snake is in fact a stick, one may take an unnecessary detour, but for the rest no real harm is done.

These error-management processes can also be applied to conspiracy theories (Van Prooijen & Van Vugt, 2018). In ancestral times, tribal warfare was common and the chance of being killed by hostile coalitions or groups (i.e., actual conspiracies) was relatively high. In such an environment, not recognizing a conspiracy that truly exists is arguably more costly than perceiving a dangerous conspiracy that does not exist. Missing a truly dangerous conspiracy after all implies a relatively high likelihood of being killed. Threatening cues in the direct environment would therefore put people on their guard for possible conspiracies, leading them to overestimate the likelihood that others are secretly conspiring for nefarious purposes.

The remnants of these evolved processes are still visible today, when people often attribute existentially threatening circumstances to the actions of hostile conspiracies. Aversive feelings such as powerlessness, loss of control, fear, or uncertainty increase people's desire to make sense of the situation that they find themselves in, and during this mental sense-making process it is natural for them to assume the worst. In doing so, people tend to be suspicious particularly of groups are powerful (and that could hence cause real harm), that are perceived as "different", and that they feel uncomfortable with—such as governmental institutions, major companies, or distrusted minority groups. As a result, people come up with conspiracy theories about the malpractice of these groups, which answers many unresolved questions that people have about the events they try to comprehend. Distressed feelings put people in a suspicious, information-seeking state-of-mind, leading them to perceive malevolent conspiracies as responsible for a range of societal events.

Much psychological research has examined the relationship between distressing circumstances and people's tendency to believe conspiracy theories. These studies have found support for a link between distress and conspiracy beliefs at various levels of analysis, including individual differences, demographics, situational factors, and macro-level societal factors. At the individual level, an impactful meta-analysis by Shauna Bowes and colleagues has identified what motivational and personological variables predict conspiracy beliefs (Bowes et al., 2023). Among the most reliable predictors of conspiracy beliefs were perceiving social threats, a tendency to perceive existential threats, and belief in a dangerous world. These are all indicators of a structural tendency to assume others are hostile, and to worry about personal safety. As these authors concluded, perceiving danger and threat are among the strongest predictors of conspiracy beliefs.

Besides such individual predispositions, people may differ in the extent to which their life circumstances are distressing. One key insight is that conspiracy beliefs are more likely among people who experience precarious, insecure life circumstances. These circumstances may include (but are not limited to) feelings of unsafety, financial problems, experiences of marginalization, and low social-economic status. Relatedly, conspiracy beliefs are more common among people with lower education levels and among people who feel powerless in society (Adam-Troian et al., 2023; Van Prooijen, 2017; Van Prooijen et al., 2018). Of importance, all these circumstances may be real and yield real problems to people. But true problems can stimulate far-fetched beliefs that are unlikely to be true. As outlined by the Existential Threat Model of Conspiracy Theories, people often try to make sense of their difficult life circumstances—why is this happening to me? Why am I not wealthy and successful? Why do I not get the respect that I deserve? In answering these questions, it is tempting to attribute these problems to powerful, hostile conspiracies that are beyond one's control. I did not do anything wrong; it's the government that's making life so difficult for me and many others, just for their own nefarious purposes!

People can feel threatened in many ways. A common distinction in psychology is between realistic versus symbolic threats. Realistic threats refer to events that might truly, and sometimes even physically, harm people: Climate change, a pandemic, an economic recession, a war. Symbolic threats, in contrast, refer to events that people may perceive as a threat to their cherished cultural or moral values. The distinction between realistic versus symbolic threats can be clarified in the arguments often voiced at the far-right against immigration. One common argument is that immigrants take away jobs and houses, increasing unemployment rates and house prices for the host population. This argument suggests that people in these far-right groups experience immigration as a realistic threat. Another common argument, however, is that people sometimes feel as if their culture is disappearing, and the traditions one got accustomed to are no longer guaranteed. This feeling that one's culture is being replaced, or changed, by outsiders would be an example of people experiencing a symbolic threat.

In a range of studies with high sample sizes, and carried out in multiple countries, we have compared the links of realistic and symbolic threats with conspiracy beliefs (Abadi et al., 2024). Our findings indicated that the type of threat did not matter much: Both realistic and symbolic threats reliably predicted conspiracy beliefs. This suggests that not the threat itself, but the negative emotions that they are associated with, stimulate conspiracy beliefs. There were exceptions to this, however, which suggests an interesting paradox: Some conspiracy theories are denialist in that they downplay the seriousness of an actual threat. Correspondingly, we did not find that experiencing the COVID-19 pandemic as threatening to own or public health was associated with increased conspiracy beliefs. This does not mean, however, that feelings of threat were unrelated to conspiracy beliefs also in this setting. A pandemic can be experienced as threatening in different ways besides health. The extent to which people experienced the pandemic as threatening to society— by harming the economy and public safety—did predict pandemic conspiracy beliefs. Even conspiracy theories that downplay an actual threat may be stimulated by other types of threat. Correspondingly, it might reasonably be expected that people who believe in conspiracy theories downplaying the reality of climate change are more likely to perceive governments, scientists, and other important institutions as deceptive.

One example of a realistic threat closely associated with climate change is natural disasters. As global warming increases, so does the extremity of the weather, increasing the likelihood of floods, tornados, and hurricanes. Moreover, some areas of the world are susceptible to occasional natural disasters for reasons unrelated to climate change, such as earthquakes. Would people who are living in areas of the world relatively high at risk for natural disasters be particularly susceptible to conspiracy theories? My PhD student Qi Zhao analyzed a global dataset conducted in 67 countries, including 47,816 participants. He coded the countries using official metrics indicating their risk for natural disasters. To the extent people lived in areas of the world higher in natural disaster risk, they were more likely to believe in conspiracy theories. Subsequent experiments suggested that this link is not inevitable: If the government was perceived as well capable of coping with natural disasters, people did not believe conspiracy theories more strongly. Only the combination of high natural disaster risk and an incapable government predicted increased conspiracy beliefs (Zhao et al., 2024). Again, distressing circumstances predict increased conspiracy beliefs, but only insofar people can blame their negative circumstances on a powerful or distrusted group they can hold responsible.

Finally, macro-level factors that are associated with how insecure citizens feel in societies predict conspiracy beliefs. One example is economic inequality. If wealth is distributed in a relatively unequal manner in societies, people are more likely to perceive society, their position in it, and their social relationships, as unstable. Perceived economic inequality therefore stimulates feelings of anomie in citizens, that is, the feeling that society is breaking down. Accordingly, perceiving societies as economically unequal increases belief in conspiracy theories (Jetten et al., 2022). Another example is how well countries perform economically. Citizens living in countries with lower GDP tend to believe conspiracy theories more strongly (Hornsey et al., 2023). Apparently, also macro-level, societal factors that plausibly predict how distressed citizens feel in their life are associated with conspiracy beliefs.

In sum, feelings of distress fuel belief in conspiracy theories. Yet, there are two complications to these effects that deserve to be noted. A first complication is that these aversive emotions do not lead to conspiracy theories amongst everyone and in every circumstance:

Sometimes distressed feelings can *increase* support for authorities. For example, many conspiracy theories emerged after the 9/11 terrorist attacks, but we should also recognize the opposite: In the months directly after the 9/11 terrorist attacks, George W. Bush was among the most positively endorsed presidents in history in terms of public approval ratings. Apparently, the 9/11 terrorist attacks not only elicited widespread conspiracy theories about the Bush-administration; it also elicited massive support for the Bush-administration. How can we reconcile this discrepancy with the present arguments?

The key here is that experiencing existential threats lead to conspiracy theories, but only if one can plausibly attribute these distressing circumstances to groups or institutions that people distrusted to begin with. Distressed feelings may actually increase support for powerful groups or institutions that people do trust. One study investigated whether or not the perception of leaders being moral or immoral influences belief in conspiracy theories. Naturally, people believe conspiracy theories more strongly about leaders that they find immoral than about leaders that they find moral. When people were led to experience uncertainty, however, these effects of morality on belief in conspiracy theories became more impactful. Put differently, uncertainty makes people endorse conspiracy theories more strongly for leaders that they find immoral, but less strongly for leaders that they find moral (Van Prooijen & Jostmann, 2013). Distressed feelings hence do not lead to indiscriminate conspiracy theorizing; it leads people to place blame on authorities, institutions, or groups that they felt uncomfortable with from the start.

A second complication is that many threatening circumstances that drive conspiracy theories imply societal change. Indeed, the feeling that society is changing rapidly in itself can be a source of distress, increasing conspiracy beliefs. But there is a paradox here: Change is exactly what many conspiracy theorists claim to desire. Belief in conspiracy theories often implies that people perceive the status quo as negative or undesirable (Federico, 2022). Accordingly, conspiracy theories are associated with activities designed to change the status quo, including activism and radical action (Imhoff et al., 2021). A possible way to reconcile this paradox is by recognizing the difference between controllable versus uncontrollable change. While speculative at this point, it stands to reason that when change is experienced as uncontrollable (and headed in an unexpected or undesired direction), people may get distressed and form conspiracy theories about the groups perceived as driving the change. But when change is experienced as controllable (e.g., because people have voted their preferred political movement in power), people are less likely to form conspiracy theories about the changes occurring in society.

DO CONSPIRACY THEORIES REDUCE DISTRESS?

Besides the Existential Threat Model, also other theoretical perspectives have recognized the role that threatening circumstances play in conspiracy theories. These include the evolutionary approach to understand the human proclivity towards conspiracy theories in distressing situations (Van Prooijen & Van Vugt, 2018), and motivational approaches to conspiracy theories (Douglas et al., 2017). All these theoretical approaches converge in a basic insight: When people feel distressed, they are more likely to turn to conspiracy theories than when they do not feel distressed. Yet, this basic insight also has yielded a lot of misunderstandings. Apparently, so many people conclude, conspiracy theories are well-suited to reduce feelings of distress and make people feel safe again. But I do not think that follows. Believing conspiracy theories is a way to cope with threatening circumstances, but not necessarily an effective coping mechanism if the goal is to feel more secure. Why would believing there are hostile conspiracies out there, seizing on every opportunity they get to harm people, increase the extent to which people feel safe?

From an evolutionary perspective, the idea that believing conspiracy theories makes people feel safe does not make sense. People evolved aversive feelings such as fear because it was adaptive to signal imminent dangers in the environment and behave in a way that avoids or neutralizes the danger. People did not evolve to just feel happy and secure as often as possible. They evolved to understand and respond to their environment in a functional manner that maximizes their chances of staying alive, or at least long enough to reproduce. From that perspective, feeling complacent and reassured after perceiving a dangerous conspiracy is not a particularly adaptive response. When perceiving a dangerous conspiracy, it would be natural to feel frightened. When danger looms in the environment, feelings of fear are useful to increase people's survival prospects. Conspiracy beliefs imply that people perceive a possibly dangerous coalition, take this danger seriously, and are ready to take appropriate action.

Indeed, the Existential Threat Model states that once formed, belief in conspiracy theories does not reduce distressed feelings; it is likely to increase them, laying the foundations for more conspiracy beliefs. Consistently, one of the most basic insights in the psychology of conspiracy theories is that belief in one conspiracy theory tends to be a good predictor of belief in a different conspiracy theory. Recall from Chapter 1 that different types of conspiracy theories exist, notably specific conspiracy theories and a generalized conspiracy mentality. These are however strongly related. Quite plausibly, accepting specific conspiracy theories as true may, over time, contribute to a general mindset that often assumes hidden conspiracies to be responsible for events happening in the world.

Research does not support the assumption that conspiracy theories make people feel safe. If anything, they make people feel more distressed. Some longitudinal studies suggest that conspiracy theories can predict increased anxiety, existential threat, and uncertainty over time (Liekefett et al., 2023). Experimental research also does not support such an effect. Overall, the evidence suggests that people are more likely to believe conspiracy theories when they feel distressed; however, these conspiracy theories are not particularly effective in subsequently reducing these aversive feelings.

3

INSIDE THE CONSPIRACY THEORIST'S MIND

People believe the strangest of things despite a complete lack of evidence. Some people believe obviously false conspiracy theories such as that the Earth is flat; or, that politicians are part of a breed of alien lizards disguised as humans, with the purpose to enslave humanity. Bizarre beliefs are not necessarily conspiratorial. Any visit to a paranormal fair will reveal groups of regular citizens—sometimes in large numbers—who believe that it is possible to predict the future by reading the lines of a person's hand, or by randomly drawing from a set of tarot cards. Telepathy is accepted as possible at these fairs, assuming that one person can read the mind of a different person no matter the physical distance between them. Mediums who claim to be able to get into contact with the souls of deceased relatives (and are able to put on a persuasive performance) can earn a fortune. When it comes to healing illnesses, people have the—often dangerous—tendency to dismiss regular medical approaches that are based on research and evidence, and instead turn to alternative approaches such as homeopathy, reiki, or spiritual healing.

All beliefs serve a similar function, which is to help people make sense of an uncertain world. After all, beliefs make assertions about unproven issues, that is, uncertainties. As we have seen in Chapter 2, conspiracy beliefs help people to make sense of distressing events by

DOI: 10.4324/9781003530718-3

providing an explanation in the form of a hostile group pulling the strings. Belief in astrology helps people make sense of an uncertain future, by making the unpredictable more predictable. Belief in the capacity of mediums to get into contact with deceased relatives helps people to make sense of what their late Uncle John has been doing recently, and whether he forgives them for all the bad things they ever did to him (if we are to believe mediums, Uncle John usually does). But how do these sense-making processes work exactly for conspiracy beliefs? This chapter will try to answer this question by examining what happens inside the conspiracy theorist's mind.

Like many other forms of belief, conspiracy beliefs are rooted in an intuitive rather than an analytic mindset. Intuitive thinking means that people rely on their gut feelings and make judgments based on automatic cognition, heuristics, and emotions. Analytic thinking means that people carefully reflect on the information that they get through complex computations. Intuitive thinking is automatic and relatively effortless; analytic thinking requires effort and concentration. Much like supernatural beliefs, conspiracy beliefs start with an intuitive first impression—a fast snap-judgment that an event cannot be understood without hidden and mysterious forces. Research indicates that a tendency towards analytic thinking—and relatedly, high education levels—predict a *decreased* likelihood of believing in conspiracy theories (Van Prooijen, 2017).

This intuitive basis of conspiracy theories may seem counterintuitive, given how articulate and carefully crafted some conspiracy theories are. Many "9/11 truth" conspiracy theories are based on a seemingly elaborate analysis of how buildings are constructed, at what temperatures steel melts, and what energy is released by the impact of a passenger plane at a certain speed. Apparently, some sort of elaborate thinking also must be involved in conspiracy beliefs. While intuition may lead people to accept a conspiracy theory as plausible, people subsequently often are motivated to find evidence to support their intuition. They engage in an extensive thinking process, but not in a neutral manner. Once people are committed to the notion that a conspiracy theory must be true, they go on a fishing expedition looking for evidence in favor of the theory—while in the process also dismissing any evidence against it. In the following, I will discuss how people accept conspiracy theories through their intuitive first impressions and highlight the specific mental processes that are relevant for these purposes. Then, I describe how people fall prey to the confirmation bias by using their analytic thinking skills to justify their conspiracy beliefs.

INTUITIVE FIRST IMPRESSIONS

Many psychological processes contribute to intuitive first impressions, but they tend to have one feature in common: The processes are fast, and may include automatic cognitive processes, heuristics, and emotional processes. Intuition refers to those impressions or judgments that come to mind without having to reason consciously about it. This section will discuss the role of two automatic cognitive processes, namely illusory pattern perception and hyperactive agency detection; of two heuristics, specifically proportionality and representativeness; and of feelings and emotions.

Illusory pattern perception

Pattern perception is the tendency of the human mind to "connect dots" and perceive meaningful and causal relationships between people, objects, animals, and events. Perceiving patterns is the opposite of perceiving randomness. Events that are random are chaotic and unpredictable; events that contain patterns, and hence are nonrandom, are understandable and predictable. The capacity of the human mind to automatically look for and find patterns is highly functional, as it enables them—amongst other things—to predict the consequences of their actions. Arguably, most people would not survive a single day without their ability to perceive patterns. I love jogging and always make a conscious decision to do this in a park. Why do I never opt for a change of scenery and decide to go jogging on a busy freeway? Because I see patterns. I understand that there is a causal and meaningful relationship between cars that drive at a high speed and the likelihood of dying if one tries to jog in their way. Jogging in the park versus on the freeway differ in a nonrandom fashion in terms of expected health consequences, and the fact that people are able to appreciate that makes them better equipped to effectively navigate the world.

Functional as it may be in most circumstances, there is one drawback to the mind's automatic tendency to look for patterns: Sometimes events truly are random, but most people perceive patterns anyway. This is referred to as *illusory pattern perception*: People sometimes see meaningful relationships that just do not exist. Such illusory pattern perception is related to many forms of beliefs, including supernatural beliefs, but also conspiracy beliefs. Interestingly, illusory pattern perception does not appear to be exclusive to humans: Traces of illusory pattern perception has been found among pigeons. The psychologist Skinner, well known for his work on operant conditioning, provided hungry pigeons with food at regular time intervals (Skinner, 1948). What he found was quite remarkable: The pigeons started doing whatever they were doing shortly before they received food in the previous trial. Apparently, the birds saw a pattern that was illusory, by connecting their behavior with the food that they received: "The last time I shook my head like this I received a nice treat, so let's try again". In fact, they would receive food at a fixed time, regardless of what they did. In the words of Skinner:

> The experiment might be said to demonstrate a sort of superstition. The bird behaves as if there were a causal relation between its behavior and the presentation of food, although such a relation is lacking.

(p. 171)

Chapter 1 has described how patterns are part of the definition of conspiracy theories, as conspiracy theories always assume (often hidden) relationships between people, objects, and events. Quite often these relationships may be obvious to those who believe the conspiracy theory, but not to those who disbelieve it. An example is the conspiracy theory that the radiation of the 5G mobile network was the reason why people were getting ill in March 2020. This theory was (amongst others) promoted by the well-known British conspiracy theorist David Icke, who asserted that it was not a coincidence that the 5G mobile network was first activated in Wuhan, China. To people who believe this conspiracy theory, these relationships (People getting ill—Wuhan—Introduction of the 5G network) may seem like hard evidence, or at least strongly suggestive facts that require an explanation. People who do not believe this conspiracy theory may be more critical of this "evidence", however, and point to the fact that besides Wuhan, the 5G network was introduced at the same time in many other Chinese cities, including places where the pandemic arrived weeks later and where (due to the restrictive measures that had been implemented in the meantime) the number of COVID-related deaths were much lower.

An interesting research question that follows from the role of patterns in conspiracy belief is this: Are people who are susceptible to conspiracy beliefs generally more likely to perceive patterns in randomness? To answer this question, I carried out a series of studies together with Karen Douglas and a student, Clara De Inocencio. We found that people who saw patterns in random coin toss outcomes were also more likely to believe conspiracy theories, as well as supernatural phenomena (Van Prooijen et al., 2018). Furthermore, we looked at the extent to which participants saw patterns in rather abstract and chaotic paintings by the American artist Jackson Pollock. These are paintings that elicit quite different reactions among modern art lovers: Some people see interesting figures, geometric figures, or beautiful sceneries in them, but others merely see paint randomly splashed on canvas. We found that the more clearly participants saw patterns in these abstract paintings, the more likely they were to believe conspiracy theories as well as supernatural phenomena.

Several studies have been conducted in the past few years to investigate this relationship further, with mixed results: The link between conspiracy beliefs and a tendency to see patterns in randomness is often, but not always found. This was resonated in a meta-analysis on these issues, showing a robust link between conspiracy beliefs and pattern perception, but on average with a small effect size (Sternisko et al., 2022). Quite possibly there are moderators to this relationship, meaning that the relationship between a tendency to see patterns in randomness and conspiracy beliefs may vary across different conspiracy theories, settings, participant groups, and cultures. More research is necessary to clarify this. Altogether, part of the sense-making processes underlying conspiracy beliefs is people's automatic tendency to detect patterns in randomness, although this is unlikely to be the only factor.

Hyperactive agency detection

Agency detection refers to people's tendency to recognize intentionality in the actions of others. Detecting agency thus means establishing that a willful agent committed an act on purpose. As with pattern perception, people's ability to detect agency is highly functional, and potentially life-saving. Imagine taking a hike through a national park in Canada, and after a few hours of enjoying all the beautiful scenery you suddenly stand face-to-face with a grizzly bear. In such cases, the ability to detect agency may well save your life. Recognizing that the bear might have certain intentions (i.e., to kill you) may lead you to take appropriate action (apparently, do NOT take a run for it as the bear is faster; instead, climbing a tree, or staying as calm as possible, is better). In many other situations it also is functional to detect agency. Think of a situation where a pedestrian is killed after a collision with a car. Did the driver do this on purpose, or was it a tragic accident? People find the answer to this question crucial to establish whether or not the driver should be punished.

Agency detection is part of a broader mental capacity called Theory of Mind: People can imagine what other people are thinking and feeling, making them understand why others behave in a certain way. Theory of Mind is indispensable to have a successful social life, because it enables people to predict the social consequences of their actions. Why do people usually not "Laugh Out Loud" at a funeral? Because they have a Theory of Mind. People understand that unstoppable laughter upon seeing the remains of the deceased person would be extremely hurtful for all the people who are mourning. Moreover, people understand that there may be long-term consequences of such laughter. It will compromise their friendships, it will ruin their reputation, and it will decrease the likelihood that others will help them in the future. Thanks to their Theory of Mind people develop a good sense of when to speak up, when to shut their mouth, when to apologize, when to turn the volume of their music a bit lower, and so on. It also enables people to understand whether an act was committed on purpose or accidentally.

But just like people make mistakes in pattern perception, they also make mistakes in agency detection: People often perceive agency where none exists, a phenomenon sometimes referred to as hyperactive agency detection. In a classic study conducted in 1944 by Fritz Heider and Marianne Simmel, participants saw two-dimensional footage of two triangles and a circle moving around at a screen and were then asked to describe what they saw. There were no computers or highly realistic animations at the time, and this footage was as basic as it gets. But that is exactly the point: Despite the fact that these utterly simplistic geometric figures clearly are not alive and have no real emotions or intentions, participants came up with stories that ascribed agency to these figures. For instance, participants would describe how the big triangle was angry at the small triangle and became aggressive, or how the circle was curious and started nosing around the big triangle's house (which was a non-moving rectangle on the screen). Agency detection is part of many forms of beliefs, such as the belief in ghosts (which assumes that deceased people still have goals), gods (assuming the existence of a supreme being that has intentions), and fate (assuming that some events were meant to happen, as part of a plan).

Agency detection is also a defining feature of conspiracy theories, as conspiracy theories always assume that a nefarious act was carried out on purpose. If a plane crashes due to technical failure or human error, conspiracy theories may assert that a secret organization willfully brought it down. Or, the conspiracy theory may assume it actually was an accident, but then still, a secret organization purposefully tries to cover up sensitive details such as a mysterious cargo that was on board. Conspiracy theories also rarely assume incompetence among the alleged conspirators. On the contrary, many conspiracy theories assume exceptional power, knowledge, and foresight among the perpetrators. To deliberately create a new virus and release it to cause the COVID-19 pandemic (as asserted in "plandemic" conspiracy theories) would require not only utter evilness, but also superhuman genius. Some conspiracy theories assume that national governments try to control human minds through wireless technology, which would involve massive coordination between governments and tech companies, and brilliant secret technology that can influence people's mind while staying undetected by critical investigators. Conspiracy theories assume a sophisticated, detailed, and intelligent plan amongst the conspirators.

Research suggests that seeing agency where none exists predicts both supernatural beliefs and conspiracy beliefs. One study recruited university students and visitors of a paranormal fair as participants. These participants watched many short movies consisting of light points that in some case would, and in other cases would not, jointly form a human walking figure. Participants could thus perceive or misperceive an intentional agent in these light points. Results revealed that as compared to university students, visitors of the paranormal fair reported more "false alarms"—that is, perceiving an intentional agent when in fact there was none (Van Elk, 2013). Moreover, such hyperactive agency detection predicted paranormal belief. As to conspiracy theories, one study included two measures of hyperactive agency detection. One was anthropomorphism, which refers to the tendency to ascribe human intentions and emotions to animals, objects, or situations. For instance, if one believes that the wind has emotions, one is anthropomorphizing the wind. As a second measure, research participants saw the famous Heider and Simmel footage, and were asked how purposeful the shapes were. Participants who perceived more agency on both measures were also more likely to believe conspiracy theories (Douglas et al., 2016). Hyperactive agency detection is part of the sense-making processes underlying conspiracy beliefs.

Heuristics

While pattern perception and agency detection are automatic cognitive processes, heuristics also are part of the intuitive mindset leading people to accept conspiracy theories. Heuristics are cognitive shortcuts, simple "rules of thumb" that people make to quickly and efficiently make sense of reality. Heuristics are functional because they often can lead to reasonably accurate conclusions without much effort; however, heuristics also make people prone to errors. Although many different heuristics exist, below I will review two heuristics that have been associated with conspiracy beliefs particularly often.

One heuristic that is relevant for conspiracy thinking is the proportionality heuristic, which refers to the assumption that a big consequence must have had a big cause. Let me illustrate the role of the proportionality heuristic in conspiracy belief with a simple and hypothetical example. A president is a human being and can die from accidents or illnesses. It is perfectly possible for an otherwise healthy president to die from a tiny flu virus, just like everyone else. Now, imagine for a moment that this would actually happen to a sitting US president, or a UK prime minister. Would many citizens believe that this event indeed was caused by a simple virus, or would they believe a conspiracy theory? Although certainly the opinions would differ among the public, and a lot would depend upon specific details of the case, in general I am quite confident that many citizens would come up with major conspiracy theories asserting that the president was murdered (or was kidnapped; or staged their own death). The explanation of an event as big as the death of a president through a cause as small as a flu virus is just hard to swallow for many people: It cannot possibly be this simple, there must be more to such an impactful, world-changing event than that. If the consequence was big, the cause must have been big as well.

The proportionality heuristic has been shown to influence people's tendency to believe conspiracy theories. Imagine that a president of a small country gets assassinated. In one case, this assassination instigates an unforeseen chain of events ultimately leading to a war. In the other case, the assassination may still be tragic but does not lead to a war. Put differently, the assassination has a big consequence (a war) or not. Who assassinated the president—was it a lone gunman, or was it a governmental conspiracy? A study revealed that participants considered a conspiracy more likely in this scenario if the assassination led to a war than if it did not lead to a war (Leboeuf & Norton, 2012). People assumed a big cause for a big consequence, which fueled a conspiracy theory. Various other studies suggest a similar principle: The more impactful and harmful a societal event is, the more likely it is that people believe in a conspiracy theory to explain it.

Proportionality is relevant for conspiracy beliefs because it helps people estimate the causes of events (and makes people prone to mistakes in establishing these causes). Besides establishing causes, however, many conspiracy theories also are about assessing probabilities: How likely is it that a conspiracy was at play? Is the chance that the coronavirus leaked from a lab bigger or smaller than the chance that it transferred from animals to humans? Several heuristics help people to quickly and effortlessly assess probabilities—and facilitate errors in doing so. One relevant heuristic for these purposes is representativeness, where people rely more on their own stereo-types than on statistics to estimate probabilities. The representative-ness heuristic can cause people to commit the conjunction fallacy, which is the erroneous tendency to estimate two events happening at the same time as more likely than one of these events happening.

A famous example of the conjunction fallacy is where people read a short paragraph about a woman (Linda) describing her as an independent, outspoken, and intelligent person who is deeply con-cerned about social justice. Subsequently, participants are asked to rate the probabilities that (a) Linda is a bank teller and (b) Linda is a bank teller *and* active in the feminist movement. Statistically speak-ing, (a) is always more probable than (b). But as the description of Linda matches a feminist, the representativeness heuristic may increase people's temptation to rate option (b) as more plausible. Various studies have indicated that conspiracy beliefs are associ-ated with a higher likelihood of committing this conjunction fal-lacy in a broad range of settings (Gagliardi, 2025). This suggests that conspiracy beliefs are related with heuristics that lead people to misjudge probabilities. Somewhat encouragingly, recent research suggests that people can be trained to avoid making the conjunction fallacy. Such conjunction fallacy training reduces people's belief in conspiracy theories, particularly after listing evidence or arguments disconfirming a conspiracy theory (Stall & Petrocelli, 2023). While such interventions need further testing, the evidence is consistent with the notion that heuristics—specifically proportionality and representativeness—are part of the sense-making processes under-lying conspiracy beliefs.

Feelings and emotions

The conspiracy theorist's mind is not only about cold and calcula-tive cognitive processes designed to find out if a conspiracy theory is true or false. Belief in conspiracy theories is to a substantial extent rooted in their feelings and emotions. Particularly negative feelings and emotions have been associated with conspiracy theories. This may also represent a heuristic, specifically the affect heuristic (Slovic et al., 2007): People base their judgments or decisions on how they feel about a particular stimulus. If people experience negative feelings or emotions towards authority figures such as politicians, managers, or journalists, they are more likely to assume that these people are involved in nefarious conspiracies.

Based on this affect heuristic, one might expect a causal effect of negative emotions on conspiracy beliefs. When looking at discrete emotions—notably anxiety and anger—the actual evidence for this is mixed at best, however. While anger and anxiety are positively correlated with conspiracy beliefs, it has turned out difficult to find a reliable, replicable causal effect of these emotions. In a 2015 study, fear increased belief in conspiracy theories but anger did not (Whitson et al., 2015). Later work, however, has found a causal effect of anger, but only among people who are angry quite frequently (i.e., trait anger) (Symaniak et al., 2023). Moreover, longitudinal studies have found no evidence for an effect of anxiety on conspiracy beliefs over time (Liekefett et al., 2023). While the number of published studies testing for a causal effect of these emotions is limited, the currently available evidence suggests that the correlations between anxiety, anger, and conspiracy beliefs may be due more strongly to conspiracy beliefs shaping these discrete emotions than vice versa.

This appears inconsistent with the notion that threatening events increase conspiracy beliefs. At least two explanations are possible to reconcile this paradox. First, the effects of threatening events may be due not to these discrete emotions but to other feelings, such as lacking control, feelings of exclusion, or feelings of powerlessness (Abalakina-Paap et al., 1999; van Prooijen & Acker, 2015; Poon et al., 2020). Second, whereas discrete emotions tend to be short-lived and tied to a specific situation (people rarely stay angry or scared for weeks in a row), a tendency to endorse conspiracy beliefs is relatively stable over time (Wang & Van Prooijen, 2023; Van Prooijen, Amodio et al., 2023). Instead of such short-lived discrete emotions, conspiracy beliefs therefore may be rooted in relatively complex feelings that often last longer—for instance feelings of powerlessness, hate, cynicism, distrust, and feeling disenfranchised. While speculative at this point, it is plausible that threatening situations may stimulate conspiracy beliefs particularly among those citizens that already experience such aversive feelings in a relatively structural manner. In line with the affect heuristic, these structurally aversive feelings may enhance the interpretation that distressing societal events were caused on purpose by hostile elites.

Moreover, not only negative emotions matter for conspiracy beliefs. Some evidence suggests that positive emotions that are commonly associated with uncertainty (i.e., hope and surprise) also predict increased conspiracy beliefs (Whitson et al., 2015). Moreover, being exposed to conspiracy theories can, in some specific circumstances, increase people's positive feelings. In one study, we asked participants to read a paragraph about the infamous sex offender Jeffrey Epstein. Half of the participants read a paragraph supporting the official narrative (Epstein committed suicide) while the other half read a popular conspiracy theory about this case (Epstein was murdered in his prison cell). Reading the conspiracy theory elicited more positive feelings than the official narrative among participants. Possibly the conspiracy theory satisfied people's need for justice to some extent: Arguably, suicide implies that Epstein managed to escape justice, but being murdered implies he still received some retribution for his acts, albeit not via the appropriate legal procedures (Van Prooijen et al., 2022).

Moreover, our work has found that conspiracy beliefs are associated more strongly with the intensity rather than the valence of emotions. Such emotional intensity is what make conspiracy theories entertaining, that is, interesting, exciting, and attention-grabbing. Indeed, in everyday life people can be entertained both through positive emotions (e.g., laughter caused by a comedian) and negative emotions (e.g., anxiety caused by a scary movie). Our studies show that people find conspiratorial narratives more entertaining than non-conspiratorial ones; and, these entertainment appraisals subsequently predict how likely people are to believe these conspiracy theories (Van Prooijen et al., 2022). Altogether, it is clear that feelings and emotions are part of the conspiracy theorist's mind, but also that more research is needed to clarify what feelings and emotions are mostly cause or consequence of conspiracy beliefs.

THE CONFIRMATION BIAS

All of the above processes help explain the intuitive first impressions that lead people to endorse a conspiracy theory but also paints an incomplete picture of the conspiracy theorist's mind. How can people maintain their conspiracy beliefs even when evidence piles up that they are wrong? Surely people who believe that the Earth is flat may at some point look out an airplane window and see the Earth's curvature with their own eyes? And people who believe that climate change is a hoax must occasionally see footage of melting icecaps, or reports of heat records being broken months in a row? People inevitably will come across evidence inconsistent with their conspiracy theories, and yet they often maintain belief in them. To understand this, one must recognize that people do engage in extensive thinking when reasoning about conspiracies, but often in a biased manner. People maintain implausible conspiracy theories through the confirmation bias: They selectively look for, support, or ignore evidence in such a manner that their suspicions are confirmed.

A classic perspective in social psychology asserts that people are motivated to maintain a coherent worldview, and experience cognitive dissonance when their beliefs are inconsistent with their actions or new information (e.g., climate change is a hoax, yet sea levels are rising) (Festinger, 1957). To resolve such cognitive dissonance people have various strategies at their disposal, which may include changing their beliefs (maybe climate change is real after all), but also, they may change how they interpret the incoming information (sea levels are not actually rising; or, climate change is real, but human activity has nothing to do with that; or, experts disagree about the question whether sea levels are rising). The more invested people are in a particular belief, the more likely it is that they are motivated to reject any information inconsistent with it.

One common metaphor to describe different modes of thinking is the distinction between the judge and the lawyer in a criminal case. Both the judge and the lawyer carefully think about the case, but they have different goals. The judge is motivated to do justice and therefore tries to neutrally and dispassionately weigh all the pieces evidence, regardless of whether they do or do not support a suspect's guilt. The lawyer, however, is motivated to get their client acquitted. The lawyer therefore invests time trying to find evidence supporting the suspects' innocence, or clues suggesting that incriminating evidence might be unreliable. When people are emotionally invested in a particular conspiracy theory, the lawyer-mode of thinking can help people resolve their cognitive dissonance and maintain belief in the theory. In doing so, people use different evidentiary standards for preferred versus unpreferred conclusions. For preferred conclusions people wonder if they *can* believe it, but for unpreferred conclusions people wonder if they *must* believe it (Epley & Gilovich, 2016). This makes changing the mind of a committed conspiracy theorist an uphill battle. People are motivated to rationalize and justify their beliefs, and therefore people sometimes dismiss even the strongest pieces of evidence showing their beliefs are mistaken.

IN CLOSING

The conspiracy theorist's mind is complicated and includes both relatively fast, intuitive thinking processes, as well as slower, more deliberative thinking processes. While the processes underlying people's intuitive first impressions support a conspiracy theory described here were not exhaustive, a key takeaway of this chapter is that automatic cognition, heuristics, and feelings and emotions, all contribute to conspiracy beliefs. This emphasis on intuitive first impressions does not preclude a role of more deliberative thinking, however, particularly when trying to maintain or prove a conspiracy theory. When people are emotionally invested in a specific conspiracy theory, they may commit the confirmation bias and selectively try to find evidence supporting their theory or discrediting non-conspiratorial explanations.

The notion that people maintain conspiracy beliefs through the confirmation bias leaves one important issue unresolved, however: Why would people become emotionally invested in a conspiracy theory to begin with? Surely there is nothing wrong with changing one's mind, particularly when confronted with new information? People change their mind about things all the time. The problem, however, is that people often tie their identity to a conspiracy theory. People sometimes become part of groups where endorsing a particular conspiracy theory is the norm, and these groups may be important to them. Or, conspiracy theories may provide convenient explanations for group failure, as is the case with allegations of election fraud ("we did not actually lose; they cheated!"). The following chapter will therefore focus on the intergroup processes that are part of belief in conspiracy theories.

4

THE SOCIAL ROOTS OF CONSPIRACY THEORIES

No US presidential election has been as polarized as the one between Joe Biden and Donald Trump in 2020. Even before all votes were counted, Donald Trump started claiming that Democrats had rigged the elections and that he was the actual winner. Following baseless conspiracy theories that involved rigged voting machines and other forms of electoral fraud, a large portion of Trump loyalist, elected Republicans, and Republican voters considered the elections results illegitimate. All of these conspiratorial allegations escalated into the 6 January 2021 Capitol Hill riots, where a mob of angry citizens stormed the Capitol in an attempt to violently overthrow the election results. This "Stop the Steal" movement underscores a basic property of conspiracy theories, namely its intergroup dimension. A conspiracy implies that a group or coalition of actors (in this case, Democrats) imposes harm by carrying out a malevolent plan that has been concocted in secret (in this case, rigging the elections). Conspiracy theories thus underscore the evil qualities of other groups.

While some studies suggest that in the US Republicans in general are more susceptible to conspiracy theories than Democrats (Van der Linden et al., 2021), this certainly does not preclude similar conspiracy theories among Democrats. In a five-wave longitudinal

DOI: 10.4324/9781003530718-4

study conducted during the 2020 elections, my PhD student Haiyan Wang indeed found that Republicans were more likely to believe that Democrats had rigged the elections in the waves *after* the results were known. Haiyan also had collected two waves *prior* to the elections, however. In these waves, Democrats were more worried that Republicans would rig the elections than vice versa (Wang & Van Prooijen, 2023). And four years later, when Trump survived an assassination attempt in Pennsylvania on 13 July 2024, the BlueAnon movement gained momentum—A Democratic counterpart of QAnon, for instance alleging that Trump had staged the assassination attempt for electoral gain. The tendency to see competing groups as evil conspirators is powerful and can be found across the political spectrum.

These intergroup processes are visible also at the geopolitical level: Conspiracy theories have played a role in countries' decision to wage war. When Putin decided to invade Ukraine in 2022, an important part of his rhetoric justifying this decision was that the Ukrainian government was a group of Nazis that committed genocide on Russian minorities. While I do not claim that such conspiracy theories were the only reason for Putin to wage war, research does support the notion that belief in these conspiracy theories predicts increased support for the war among the public (Šrol & Čavojová, 2024). Moreover, throughout history wars have been started following conspiratorial allegations about other nations. When Hitler invaded the Soviet Union in 1941, historians agree that he had at least two motivations for this decision. The first was simple greed in the form of conquering more territory for the Third Reich ("Lebensraum"). But the second reason was the belief that communism was a Jewish conspiracy for world domination. All of these examples underscore the social roots of conspiracy theories, suggesting they can fuel intergroup conflict.

These social roots are reflected in the basic structure of any conspiracy theory. A conspiracy is by definition a coalition or a group, consisting of, for instance, politicians, political institutions,

CEOs, major companies, ethnic or religious groups, and the like. Sometimes the suspected conspirators may not even be human—think of AI-conspiracy theories (where hostile computer systems try to enslave humanity, like in the movie "the Matrix"), or conspiracy theories that alien lizards dress up like humans to oppress people. But even then, conspiracy theories always assume a group of deliberate actors with evil motives. Also, these conspiracies often do not just plot against a perceiver personally—they plot against a wider collective of people, such as citizens, employees, patients, or the perceiver's ethnic or religious group. Conspiracy theories imply that "they" are threatening to harm or deceive "us"—whomever "they" and "us" might refer to exactly.

To understand these social roots of conspiracy theories, in the following I discuss what conspiracy theories imply for people's own identity, and what they imply for how people perceive other groups (Van Prooijen, 2024). First, through a variety of processes conspiracy theories can help people develop, maintain, and protect a positive social identity. This positive social identity can lead people to become entrenched in their beliefs, stimulating the motivated reasoning processes described in Chapter 3. But also, this positive identity can fuel feelings of group superiority, thus providing people with a sense of entitlement during conflicts with other groups (e.g., "America First"). Second, through concrete allegations of misconduct conspiracy theories underscore the hostile qualities of a different group. Such demonization promotes feelings of outgroup threat and can justify intergroup hostilities, sometimes even including violence.

CONSPIRACY THEORIES AS A SOURCE OF IDENTITY

The QAnon movement started in 2017 in the US and gradually attracted followers also in other countries. QAnon is a far-right political movement that endorses a wide set of different conspiracy theories. The basic premise of QAnon is that a mysterious figure named "Q" had access to the highest level of national security information during the first Trump presidency. Q left clues on online message boards to inform followers of what was going on behind the scenes. According to Q, Donald Trump was trying to dismantle a Deep State of left-wing Democratic elites who were involved in all sorts of nefarious activities. QAnon is particularly well-known for its blood libel accusations, suggesting that Democratic elites sexually exploit children, drink their blood, and perform Satanic rituals on them.

For the present purposes, it is important to realize that a movement like QAnon can become a central part of the identity of its followers. QAnon unites followers with group symbols; specifically, the letter "Q" has been regularly spotted at Trump rallies. The movement also has mottos designed to increase cohesion and give members a collective purpose ("Where we go one, we go all"). This example underscores that conspiracy theories can be a source of people's identity: "QAnon is not just a movement; it is part of who I am". Once people start identifying themselves with their conspiracy beliefs or become members of groups where belief in conspiracy theories is a strong norm, changing their minds becomes rather difficult. People may accept critical feedback for ideas that are not particularly important to them, but they are less likely to accept criticism of ideas that define who they are.

Together with a group of colleagues, we became a member of a range of Dutch anti-vaccination Telegram groups (Schlette et al., 2023). While conspiracy theories are not the only reason why people may develop anti-vaccination sentiments, belief in conspiracy theories does tend to be strongly associated with anti-vaccination attitudes and behaviors (Hornsey et al., 2018; Loomba et al., 2021; Van Prooijen & Böhm, 2023). In these groups, we did not intervene or post messages; we only observed. Our key question was: What are the users in these groups talking about? One might expect that people use these platforms mostly to organize online or offline protests for their cause. We found that this indeed was part of their discussions, but not the most important part. To a larger extent, people engage in community building on these platforms by emphasizing a shared identity. For instance, people would describe what they had in common with other members, call for emotional support, or disparage what they saw as outgroups (e.g., medical authorities). Also, as is common in community building, people used these platforms to keep each other informed of new developments (although in these particular groups a lot of information that people shared boiled down to misinformation). In sum, people were mostly looking to connect with like-minded others and keep each other informed. Just like any other belief or activity—political orientation, soccer, chess, gardening, and so on—similar interests can unite people, and conspiracy theories are no exception.

CONSPIRACY THEORIES TO MAINTAIN A POSITIVE IDENTITY

One basic insight in psychology is that people are motivated to acquire or maintain a positive self-esteem. As the groups that are part of people's identity reflect on their self-esteem, people seek to maintain a positive identity by engaging in ingroup favoritism: People emphasize the positive features of their own groups, and often believe their own groups are superior on important dimensions compared with other groups. Regardless of whether people are members of conspiratorial movements such as QAnon, conspiracy beliefs can contribute to such ingroup favoritism. Emphasizing that other groups are involved in nefarious conspiracies underscores their immoral qualities. And when other groups are immoral, it follows that our own group is morally superior, in other words, consisting of better people.

Not all forms of ingroup positivity necessarily are bad or destructive. There are "healthy" forms of identification that do not imply a negative perception of different groups. People for instance can be proud of their country while still respecting other countries, recognizing the beauty of different cultures, and without believing that their country should have special rights at the expense of other countries. A more harmful form ingroup positivity, however, is collective narcissism: An exaggerated belief in the superiority of one's own group. Nationalist movements often propagate such ingroup superiority, typically claiming that their own nation is "the greatest country on earth". Such collective narcissism damages people's relationships with other groups: Collective narcissism is associated with prejudice, conflict between groups, and support for radical movements (Golec de Zavala et al., 2019). When people believe their own group to be superior, it logically implies a belief that other groups are inferior. These perceptions of inferiority may include the belief that other groups are *morally* inferior, up to the extent that they would be part of evil conspiracies to harm the "great" ingroup.

Such collective narcissism has proven to be a reliable predictor of people's tendency to believe conspiracy theories. In a four-wave longitudinal study conducted during the 2016 US presidential campaign, collective narcissism predicted a growth in general conspiracy beliefs (attributing political events to the actions of unspecified groups) over time (Golec de Zavala & Federico, 2018). Moreover, a large-scale multi-nation study conducted in 56 countries during the pandemic examined the link between COVID-19 conspiracy beliefs and national narcissism, that is, an exaggerated belief in the greatness of one's own nation. National narcissism was positively associated with conspiracy beliefs across countries, and with a willingness to disseminate conspiracy theories (Sternisko et al., 2023).

While research on collective narcissism is mostly correlational, also experimentally exposing people to conspiracy theories can increase ingroup favoritism. My PhD student Jiayan Mao has conducted a study where he exposed US and Chinese participants to the conspiracy theory that the US government had secret, shady deals with the pharmaceutical company Pfizer during the COVID-19 pandemic (Mao et al., 2023). Subsequently he asked them to indicate their system-justifying beliefs, that is, their beliefs that the political system governing their own society is fair and legitimate.

Unsurprisingly, when US participants read about the conspiracy theory that their own government was involved in malevolent conspiracies, they rated their own US societal system as less fair and legitimate. More interesting, however, was how the Chinese participants responded. When Chinese participants read that the US government was involved in malevolent conspiracies, they rated their own Chinese societal system as fairer and more legitimate. "Their government is so bad; they conspire with pharmaceutical companies at the expense of public health! This would never happen here and shows how good our own system works". Conspiracy theories can increase ingroup favoritism by emphasizing the immoral qualities of outgroups, thus helping people to maintain a positive social identity.

CONSPIRACY THEORIES TO PROTECT A POSITIVE SOCIAL IDENTITY

Sometimes status threats can undermine people's positive social identity. How to maintain a belief in the superiority of one's own group when another group is clearly doing better? It is hard to claim that one's group is the best in a competition when it gets beaten by another group. In such cases, conspiracy theories can help to protect a positive identity: The loss in the competition is not attributed to failure of one's own group, but to foul play of the other group: "We did not actually lose; they cheated". This ego-defensive mechanism clearly seemed to be at work in the Stop the Steal movement, as Trump refused to acknowledge defeat and insisted that the Democratic party had committed election fraud. Also in the weeks prior to the 2024 elections, Trump implied that he could only lose if Kamala Harris and her team played unfairly. At a rally in Wisconsin a few weeks before the elections, he said: "They're going to cheat. They cheat. That's all they want to do is cheat. It's the only way they're going to win. And we can't let that happen, and we can't let it happen again. We're going to have no country".

More generally, conspiracy theories increase among supporters of political candidates that lose an election (Kim et al., 2022). These ego-defensive processes are not restricted to politics, however. People also use conspiracy theories to protect their identity when their favorite soccer team loses. An interesting case in point is the 2018 FIFA world cup soccer in Russia. This was the first major soccer tournament where the VAR (Video Assistant Referee) was introduced. The introduction of the VAR also led to numerous conspiracy theories, mostly involving allegations that the VAR is a form of racism designed to favor teams from traditional soccer countries (from Europe and South America) at the expense of teams from African and Middle Eastern countries. In a project led by Paul Bertin, we analyzed conspiracy tweets about the VAR during the course of the tournament (Bertin et al., 2023). Our results showed a large spike of conspiracy tweets specifically at the end of the group phase: The time when half of the teams were excluded from the tournament. Moreover, these conspiracy tweets were particularly common among supporters of teams that just had been excluded in a match where a VAR decision had played a significant role.

Also interesting was the language that these tweeters used: Conspiracy tweets contained a relatively high proportion of group-level self-categorizations, as reflected by pronouns in the first person plural ("we"; "our"; "ourselves"). This is quite remarkable, as it is opposite to a basic and well-replicated effect in social psychology. People tend to associate their identity with groups that are winning, which is referred to as "Basking in Reflected Glory" (*"We won!"*). When a group is losing, however, they tend to disassociate their identity from it, referred to as "Cutting off Reflected Failure" (*"They lost!"*). But apparently, this basic effect does not occur when people blame the loss of their team on a hostile conspiracy. In that case, "we" stand behind "our" team that has been robbed of a well-deserved victory through unfair means. Conspiracy theories keep people's identities tied to a group, even when it is losing.

Losing elections or soccer matches are incidental identity threats that people may need to cope with occasionally, when they happen. By a similar token, however, conspiracy theories also help people make sense of more structural forms of adversity in life. Why can't I get ahead like others do? Why is my life so miserable? Conspiracy theories provide people with an opportunity to externally attribute their negative life circumstances, or the injustices they perceive, to evil conspiracies, thus helping them to make sense of their situation. "The reason why I can't get ahead is because I, like many other people, are victim of a conspiracy of evil elites that seek to enrich themselves and oppress the people". Accordingly, research has shown that living in precarious circumstances, feelings of injustice, and perceived inequality predicts increased conspiracy beliefs (Adam-Troian et al., 2023; Jetten et al., 2022; Van Prooijen, 2022). Conspiracy theories are more common among groups that have a history of victimization (Pantazi et al., 2022). Cross-culturally, citizens living in countries with worse economic prospects (i.e., lower GDP) are more likely to believe conspiracy theories (Hornsey et al., 2023).

An interesting case in point is marginalized minority groups in society. These are societal subgroups that often suffer from real problems including discrimination, poverty, and inequality. What is also common in these groups, however, is conspiracy theories that offer rather unrealistic explanations for these real problems. For example, conspiracy theories involving a plot by the White majority to harm or kill Black citizens are popular among African Americans. In a study among 500 African Americans, substantial numbers believed in variants of the conspiracy theory that the White majority strategically uses birth control to limit the Black population (Thorburn & Bogart, 2005). For instance, 37.4% of the sample agreed with the statement "Medical and public health institutions use poor and minority people as guinea pigs to try out new birth control methods". Likewise, 24.8% agreed to "Poor and minority women are sometimes forced to be sterilized by the government". Such conspiracy beliefs predicted negative attitudes towards contraceptives. Some of these birth control conspiracy beliefs—specifically conspiracy theories about the safety of contraceptive methods—even predicted decreased contraceptive use among men. These conspiracy theories hence increase the risk of unwanted pregnancies and STDs.

One study compared Black versus White US college students' beliefs in 13 conspiracy theories describing how the US government deliberately and selectively harms African Americans (Crocker et al., 1999). Examples were the conspiracy theories that the government makes sure that drugs are available in Black neighborhoods; that the government deliberately creates high rates of homelessness among Black people; or that the government deliberately assigns the death penalty more to Black as opposed to White males. Black participants overwhelmingly believed all of these theories more strongly than White participants. Furthermore, belief in these conspiracy theories was to some extent due to the real problems that the African American community faces. The more strongly participants attributed their actual problems to prejudice and discrimination, the more likely they were to believe these conspiracy theories. Again, please note that many of these attributions may be justified: Prejudice and discrimination of minority groups is common, and contributes to real problems such as unemployment, poverty, and crime. But when making sense of these negative life circumstances, realistic problems can easily inspire explanations that involve unrealistic conspiracy theories.

Together with my collaborators Jaap Staman and Andre Krouwel, we further tested these effects in a Dutch sample by comparing Muslims with non-Muslims (Van Prooijen et al., 2018). Consistent with other studies, we found that Muslims were more likely than non-Muslims to believe conspiracy theories that are relevant for their Muslim identity. These included Muslim conspiracy theories (e.g., asserting that ISIS was created by the US and Israel to create chaos in the Middle East and make Islam look bad) and Jewish conspiracy theories (e.g., asserting that the Holocaust was largely made up to secure the state of Israel). More interesting, however, was that Muslims also were more likely to believe conspiracy theories largely *unrelated* to their identity. These included economic conspiracy theories (e.g., asserting that the 2007 economic crisis was caused deliberately by bankers to enrich themselves) and a range of other, well-known conspiracy theories (e.g., about the moon landings being fake, or the US government hiding evidence for the existence of extraterrestrial life).

Why did our Muslim participants even believed those conspiracy theories that ostensibly had nothing to do with them more strongly than our non-Muslim participants? Consistent with other studies, the key variable explaining our findings were feelings of deprivation, both personal (the belief that one is not seen as a full-fledged member of Dutch society) and group-based (the belief that Muslims in the Netherlands are marginalized). When people, and the groups they identify with, experience real problems, they may blame them on powerful conspiracies by seeing the system as rigged against them. And when the system is rigged against them, it is not unreasonable to assume that it is rigged also in many other ways—including a willingness to deceive the public by pretending that humans landed on the moon, or to cover up a UFO that landed near Roswell. Conspiracy theories help people make sense of their marginalized position; this may protect their positive social identity but also opens the door to a range of other, unrelated conspiracy theories.

PERCEIVED OUTGROUP THREAT

This chapter so far mostly has discussed the implications of conspiracy theories for how people feel about their own groups. Conspiracy theories also have implications for how people perceive, and feel about different groups, however. There is another core element to the social roots of conspiracy theories, which is its association with perceived outgroup threat. This association most likely consists of two, not mutually exclusive causal pathways. First, by blaming nefarious acts on other groups, conspiracy theories make these groups seem dangerous or deceptive. This has implications for the trust that people have in these groups. For example, anti-vaccination conspiracy theories may decrease the trust that people have in health authorities, making them more skeptical of other, unrelated, pieces of advice from these same authorities. Shortly after the COVID-19 pandemic, an interesting conspiracy theory gained momentum alleging that medical authorities lie not only about vaccines but also about the benefits of sunscreen. According to these theories sunscreen damages people's health, and natural, unprotected exposure to sun light (which actually can cause skin cancer) is necessary for people's health. Relatedly, in the Netherlands it was remarkable how some of the exact same influencers spreading conspiracy theories about COVID-19 started siding with Russia after its invasion of Ukraine, alleging that the press does not paint an honest picture of the war. If authorities lie to us about the pandemic, apparently, they will also lie to us about other issues.

The opposite causal pathway is also plausible, however. Recall from Chapter 3 that people use motivated reasoning (e.g., the confirmation bias) to construe a coherent view of the world. People may use conspiracy theories for that purpose. Conspiracy theories can justify the negative sentiments that people already had about different groups. It is no coincidence that Republicans are more likely to believe theories suggesting that Democrats are conspiring, and vice versa. Republicans are more likely to believe theories that Obama forged his birth certificate, or that liberal scientists lie about the dangers of global warming; conversely, Democrats are more likely to believe that 9/11 was an inside job by the (Republican) administration that was in power when it happened, and that this same administration was motivated by oil interests to start the war in Iraq (Miller et al., 2016; Smallpage et al., 2017). Conspiracy theories make abstract feelings of distrust concrete, by providing specific examples underscoring why a distrusted outgroup is a threat and should not be trusted.

Many studies underscore the link between conspiracy theories and negative perceptions of other groups. Conspiracy theories are associated with different forms of prejudice, including anti-Semitism (Kofta et al., 2020), negative sentiments towards immigrants (Jolley et al., 2020), and anti-Americanism among Europeans (Imhoff & Bruder, 2014). Moreover, conspiracy theories are associated with personality traits that predict prejudice towards different groups, notably authoritarianism and social dominance orientation (Swami, 2012). And as noted in Chapter 2, both realistic and symbolic intergroup threats reliably predict belief in conspiracy theories (Abadi et al., 2024).

During the 2019 US–China trade war, a Chinese student (Mengdi Song) and I conducted a study about intergroup conspiracy theories between these two nations, which have had a difficult relationship with each other throughout the years (Van Prooijen & Song, 2021). Among American participants, we asked a range of questions assessing their beliefs that Chinese institutions are conspiring against the US; among Chinese participants, we asked a similar range of questions assessing their beliefs that US institutions are conspiring against China. Consistent with the earlier discussed role of maintaining a positive social identity, collective narcissism predicted such intergroup conspiracy beliefs; above and beyond that, however, perceiving the other nation as a threat also contributed to these intergroup conspiracy beliefs. Believing that one's own nation is superior, while also believing that another nation is a threat, is a recipe for conflict between groups—and jointly, good predictors of conspiracy beliefs among citizens of these two nations.

A study conducted in Indonesia has attempted to find a causal effect of group identity and perceived outgroup threat on conspiracy beliefs (Mashuri & Zaduqisti, 2015). As Indonesia is the largest Muslim country in the world, the study focused on how the West might be threatening to Muslims. Half of the participants read a newspaper article describing how the threat posed by Western countries to the Muslim world has been increasing in the past decades (high outgroup threat); the other half read a newspaper article describing how this threat has been decreasing in the past decades (low outgroup threat). Furthermore, half of the participants were requested to write a brief essay describing the nature and importance of their identity as a Muslim; the other half of the participants wrote a more neutral essay about their daily activities. Results indicated that participants endorsed stronger conspiracy theories about Western involvement in Indonesian terrorism in the high as opposed to low outgroup threat condition. This effect only occurred among participants who had written an essay about their Muslim identity, however. Put differently, the description of the West as threatening increased belief in conspiracy theories, but only among Indonesian citizens who were reminded of their Muslim identity. These findings underscore the social roots of conspiracy theories: The combination of strong identification with one's own community and perceiving different groups as threatening make people susceptible to conspiracy theories.

CONCLUDING REMARKS

Conspiracy theories have a clear social dimension. A conspiracy is a hostile coalition or outgroup; and most conspiracy theories specify how the suspected conspiracy harms or deceives a larger collective of people. In this chapter we have seen that both identity-based concerns for one's own social groups (notably developing, maintaining, and protecting a positive social identity) and a perception of another group as threatening, may contribute to belief in conspiracy theories. Conspiracy theories are associated with people's natural tendency to classify the world into "we" versus "they", and conspiracy theories make suspicious feelings about other groups concrete by placing blame on them for distressing events, or by accusing them of specific ways in which they plan to harm or deceive the ingroup.

These intergroup implications of conspiracy theories are not without consequences, however. As concerns for an ingroup identity and perceived outgroup threat are closely associated with conflict between groups, conspiracy theories mobilize group members and prepare them for intergroup conflict. Conspiracy theories therefore polarize people's attitudes about other groups and ultimately might contribute to various forms of radical action, focused on damaging the interests of other groups. Belief in conspiracy theories is therefore closely coupled with radicalism. The following chapter will focus on the link between conspiracy theories and radicalism more extensively.

5

CONSPIRACY THEORIES AND RADICALISM

In 2023, the Dutch General Intelligence and Security Service (AIVD) published a report estimating that over 100,000 Dutch citizens believe in a conspiratorial narrative asserting the existence of an "evil elite" that aims to oppress and enslave the people (AIVD, 2023). This evil elite is potentially willing to kill citizens on a large scale to reach their goals, and therefore, extreme measures may be necessary to stop them. Such anti-institutional extremism can take various different (and sometimes partially overlapping) forms. For instance, some citizens endorse blood libel theories (also propagated by QAnon) that evil elites perform satanic rituals on children. Some far-right movements suggest that evil elites try to control people's everyday life by imposing "woke" values on them. The "evil elite" conspiracy theory gained momentum during the COVID-19 pandemic, where some citizens interpreted the restrictive measures to contain the spread of the virus, as well as policy pressuring citizens to get vaccinated, as manifestations of elite oppression. Also, some citizens saw the "Great Reset" proposal at the World Economic Forum (a rather abstract, unspecified proposal in 2020 by then-Prince Charles and Klaus Schwab to rebuild the world economy in a more sustainable manner after the pandemic) as direct evidence for the evil intentions of those elites. The AIVD has highlighted

DOI: 10.4324/9781003530718-5

two dangers associated with such anti-institutional extremism: These conspiracy beliefs undermine the rule of law, and also, they may inspire violence, including violent protests or targeted assaults against people seen as part of the "evil elites".

These issues relate to some of the processes discussed in the last chapter: Conspiracy theories can demonize other groups by highlighting their deceptive or immoral qualities through concrete allegations of misconduct. Conspiracy theories therefore can polarize people and ultimately may legitimize violence, particularly against the groups accused of conspiring. In this case, conspiracy theories about "societal elites" (admittedly a rather vague, catch-all term for any societal group with some sort of power) may legitimize radical action against those elites. But radicalization is associated with conspiracy theories about a broad range of societal groups. Antisemitic conspiracy theories are common across various types of radical movements. Far-right-extremists often endorse conspiracy theories about minority groups, such as immigrants and Muslims. Far-left extremists often endorse conspiracy theories about multinationals and bankers. And Islamic fundamentalist groups (e.g., ISIS; Hamas) often propagate theories about the "imperialist West" seeking to oppress Muslims.

Conspiracy beliefs thus are closely associated with radicalism, where people hold relatively extreme political or ideological beliefs, sometimes coupled with relatively extreme behavior. The extremity of such beliefs and behaviors may be seen on a scale, ranging from relatively mundane manifestations such as supporting a populist movement or engaging in minor forms of civic disobedience (e.g., not complying to regulations imposed by the government; breaking rules as a sign of protest) to truly radical manifestations such as membership of terrorist organizations and committing extremist violence. This chapter will examine the links between conspiracy theories and various forms of extremist beliefs and behaviors. To do so, the chapter will discuss (a) the links of conspiracy beliefs with populism and politically extreme attitudes; (b) the implications of belief in conspiracy theories for the rule of law; and (c) the implications of belief in conspiracy theories for extremist violence.

POPULISM AND EXTREME POLITICAL BELIEFS

Around the world, populist movements have been quite successful in elections during the past decade. These include Donald Trump and his MAGA movement, various populist parties in Europe (e.g., PVV in the Netherlands; Fidesz in Hungary; Smer in Slovakia), and populist movements in Latin-America and Asia (e.g., Bolsonaro in Brazil; Milei in Argentina; Modi in India). Populism is commonly defined as a worldview or rhetorical style that describes society as an ongoing struggle between "the people" versus "the elites" (Müller, 2016). This definition includes the elements of anti-elitism and people-centrism. Anti-elitism means that populist movements typically have an aversion against political elites (often mainstream politicians), and often also against societal elites such as scientists, CEOs, journalists, or bankers. People-centrism means that regular, hard-working citizens—and not politicians—are a focal point of attention in populist rhetoric, arguing that "the people" should ultimately be in charge of important decisions. On the surface, such people-centrism seems in line with enlightened democratic values, but in practice, it usually is not: Anti-pluralism is also part of the populist worldview, referring to the assumption that only populist movements represent the true voice of the people. Put differently, only those who support the populist leader are considered part of "the people"; all the others are considered part of "the elites" or have been misled by them. There is nothing democratic about putting only those in charge that happen to agree with a populist leader while trying to silence all the rest, sometimes even portraying other-minded people as traitors.

The populist style—emphasizing the antagonism between "the elites" and "the people"—can be found across the political spectrum, from the far-left to the far-right. Populism has little unique ideological elements and has been referred to as a "thin-layered" or "hollow" ideology (Mudde, 2004). The populist style therefore can be attached to various host ideologies such as socialism (e.g., radical socialist parties in the EU) and conservatism (e.g., MAGA). Due to these different host ideologies, there are clear differences between left-wing versus right-wing populist movements. Right-wing populist movements usually put a premium on reducing immigration and tend to be more authoritarian; left-wing populist movements tend to be skeptical about globalization and often are concerned with the power of large, multinational companies. But the elements of anti-elitism and people-centrism are visible in any populist movement.

The perceived antagonism between "the elites" versus "the people" implies a worldview characterized by intergroup conflict, where particularly societal elites are seen as dangerous or deceptive outgroups. Considering the arguments in Chapter 4, it therefore stands to reason that populist attitudes are associated with belief in conspiracy theories. Many studies indeed found a positive correlation between populist attitudes and conspiracy beliefs. We have found evidence for a link between populist attitudes and conspiracy mentality in 13 EU countries, although the strength of this relationship varied substantially between countries. The link between populism and conspiracy beliefs appeared stronger in Western-European countries than Eastern-European countries, which might be due to a range of societal, historical, or cultural differences. The relationship between populist attitudes and conspiracy beliefs was significantly positive in every country that we tested, however (Van Prooijen, Cohen Rodrigues et al., 2022).

There are multiple more specific reasons why populist attitudes and conspiracy beliefs are so closely related. One is a desire for clarity. Populist politicians often use catchy one-liners and therefore are praised by their supporters for "telling it like it is". These catchy one-liners in fact offer simplistic solutions for the relatively complex problems that a country faces. Endorsing populist leaders may hence originate from a desire for clarity—and conspiracy theories provide such clarity. After all, conspiracy theories offer comprehensive explanations for complex events. Even relatively complicated conspiracy theories often are quite simplistic in their essence, as they ultimately attribute harmful societal events largely to the deliberate actions of a hostile outgroup. Both populist attitudes and conspiracy beliefs indeed are associated with a belief in simple solutions for complex problems (Erisen et al., 2021). Relatedly, populist attitudes and conspiracy beliefs are both rooted in gullibility, as for instance reflected in a tendency to see deeper meaning in a series of nonsense statements (Van Prooijen, Cohen Rodrigues et al., 2022).

Furthermore, political cynicism, feelings of powerlessness, and perceiving life as a zero-sum game (which means assuming that if someone gains someone else loses, thus implying an antagonistic perception of social relationships) have been found to mediate the link between populism and conspiracy theories (Papaioannou et al., 2023). Finally, populism and conspiracy theories may be connected due to their entertainment value. Populist leaders quite often are rather eccentric figures who draw attention by stirring up the established political order, and admittedly are masters at finding the spotlight. Recent research suggests that these features—that some citizens might find entertaining—have an electoral function: Populism has been described as a form of "popcorn politics", meaning that support for populist leaders depends on how entertaining people find them, more so than support for non-populist leaders (Van Prooijen, Kipperman et al., 2025). As noted in earlier chapters, people tend to find conspiracy theories entertaining as well. Spreading conspiracy theories may thus help populist leaders electorally among some groups of citizens.

While populist movements occur across the political spectrum, they are most common at the far-left and the far-right. Such political extremism is a different way of examining the link between radical beliefs and belief in conspiracy theories. Are conspiracy theories more common at both extremes than among political moderates? Some studies have indeed found a "U-shape" in various European countries, suggesting stronger conspiracy beliefs at the far-left and far-right than in the center (Van Prooijen et al., 2015; Krouwel et al., 2017). This U-shape is not found universally, however. For instance, while the U-shape emerges for conspiracy theories about powerful groups, conspiracy theories about vulnerable minority groups (e.g., immigrants) tend to be prominent mostly at the far-right (Nera et al., 2021; see also Mao et al., 2024). Moreover, various studies find stronger conspiracy belief at the right than at the left, as for instance reflected in higher general conspiracy mentality among Republicans than Democrats in the US (Van der Linden et al., 2021; Wang & Van Prooijen, 2023).

Do conspiracy beliefs occur mostly at the political right, or at both political extremes? Together with a large group of conspiracy belief researchers (led by Roland Imhoff), we have investigated the relationship between political ideology and conspiracy mentality in 26 countries, based on the responses of over 100,000 participants (Imhoff et al., 2022). Our findings showed a complicated picture. It turns out not to be strictly "either-or": Conspiracy mentality is indeed stronger at both extremes than in the political center, however, overall is does seem more prominent at the far right than at the far left. The link between political ideology and conspiracy mentality thus appears to be a U-shape, but not a symmetrical one; the relationship often may look more like a "Nike-swoosh" pattern or a fishhook. This was the pattern on average, however, and there were vast differences between countries. For instance, while conspiracy mentality was stronger at the right than at the left overall, this was not a universal finding (e.g., in Spain it was stronger at the left). The policy domains in which people were left-wing or right-wing also mattered: Being economically left-wing or right-wing was not related to conspiracy mentality, however, being culturally right-wing (which implies a preference for one's own cultural values and a rejection of immigrants) was clearly associated with stronger conspiracy mentality.

Altogether, radical political beliefs seem to be associated with belief in conspiracy theories. Many studies have found conspiracy beliefs to be related with populist attitudes, and with a far-left or far-right political ideology. At the same time, it is important to recognize that the link between radical political beliefs and conspiracy beliefs is not particularly straightforward. The strength of the relationships between populist attitudes, political extremism, and conspiracy beliefs differs between countries. Moreover, the type of conspiracy theory that people believe in makes a difference, as some conspiracy theories appeal more to left-wing radicals, other conspiracy theories more to right-wing radicals, and yet others to both extremes. Finally, while overall conspiracy beliefs seem most common among right-wing political movements, this is not an effect that occurs universally, and conspiracy theories also can be quite common among left-wing political movements.

THE RULE OF LAW

While many differences exist between radical movements, most of these movements share anti-establishment sentiments and believe that existing democratic institutions are illegitimate. Moreover, extreme beliefs are associated with strong conviction in the moral righteousness of one's cause, promoting the belief that the "ends justify the means", thus justifying unlawful acts (Skitka, 2010). These notions are reflected in many conspiracy theories, accusing powerful democratic institutions of foul play, which may legitimize one to disobey the rules of those institutions. Conspiracy theories therefore have implications for the extent to which citizens respect the rule of law. Specifically, conspiracy theories are associated with rule-violations and criminal behavior. Moreover, the rule of law is closely coupled with the ideals of democracy, and conspiracy beliefs may lead citizens to reject democratic values.

One period in which the link between conspiracy beliefs and rule violations were particularly visible was the COVID-19 pandemic.

Together with a group of political scientists, we have fielded a large survey in the Netherlands among more than 9000 participants shortly after the start of the pandemic (April 2020) (Van Prooijen, Etienne et al., 2023). In this survey, participants indicated their belief in a range of COVID-19 conspiracy theories (e.g., theories that the virus had been created in the lab as a bioweapon). Then, we fielded another survey among the same participants in December 2020, and more than 5000 of the original participants again responded to our questionnaire. Our results indicated that conspiracy beliefs in April 2020 prospectively predicted participants' rule violations in the months that followed. Stronger conspiracy beliefs predicted a decreased likelihood of ignoring the restrictive measures to curb the spread of the virus. Participants specifically were more likely to indicate that they had received more visitors in their house than allowed, and to have visited a party or bar where it was more crowded than allowed, to the extent their conspiracy beliefs were stronger at the beginning of the pandemic. Conspiracy beliefs also had implications for participants' willingness to follow the health advice of medical authorities. Stronger conspiracy beliefs at the beginning of the pandemic predicted a decreased likelihood that participants would get tested for COVID-19 in subsequent months. These defiant behaviors presumably were not without consequences: If participants got tested, the test was more likely to turn out positive to the extent participants believed conspiracy theories more strongly.

Of course, these implications for ignoring medical advice and rule violations took place in a rather unusual period in recent history. Moreover, the transgressions (e.g., not practicing physical distancing) could be seen as relatively minor and represent otherwise normal behaviors that were illegal only during the lockdowns. What about actual criminal behavior? One study examined the effects of being exposed to conspiracy theories on smaller forms of property crime. British participants specifically read a text about the conspiracy theory that the British government was involved in the death of Princess Diana, and they were compared with participants who did not read any text. If participants had been exposed to a conspiracy theory, they reported a higher willingness to commit smaller forms of financial crime, such as hiding or not disclosing faults of second-hand items they were selling or filing claims they were not entitled to (Jolley et al., 2019). Conspiracy theories promote a relatively negative view of society and therefore make people less willing to respect the rules of that society.

A conspiratorial movement where the link with criminal behavior is especially visible is the sovereign citizen movement. This movement consists of people that have such strong anti-establishment sentiments, fueled by conspiracy theories, that they no longer wish to be part of society. Members of this movement fill out a few forms online to end their "contract" with the state and declare themselves "sovereign". After doing so, they believe that the law no longer applies to them. One may guess the consequences of these pseudo-legal beliefs for the willingness of sovereign citizens to obey the law. Many sovereign citizens routinely commit traffic violations, believe that they do not have to pay their bills, commit tax fraud and other forms of financial crime, print their own fake ID document from the Internet to use it as a formal identification document, and past a fake diplomat-sticker on their car (indicating they have diplomatic immunity and hence can park their car wherever they want to, without having to pay parking bills). Unsurprisingly, many sovereign citizens inevitably get in trouble with a bailiff or the police, and in some cases even get evicted from their homes after not having paid rent or mortgage for months. Some sovereign citizens respond with reactionary violence in such encounters, expressing severe feelings of injustice as they believe their basic rights as a sovereign citizen have been violated (Fiebig & Koehler, 2022; Rathje, 2022).

Besides rule-violation and criminal behavior, conspiracy beliefs have implications for how people think and feel about democracy. After all, if democracy has provided citizens with an evil and corrupt government, then there must be something fundamentally wrong with the system. It would be a mistake to portray conspiracy theorists as completely undemocratic, however. Belief in conspiracy theories is associated with a rejection of the system of representative democracy, in which citizens elect public officials to represent them in parliament or congress. However, belief in conspiracy theories is also associated with increased *support* for a system of direct democracy, in which citizens can circumvent politicians by making important policy decisions directly via referenda (Pantazi et al., 2022).

One could interpret these findings as evidence that conspiracy theorists also are democratic and just favor different forms of democratic governance. That would not be accurate either, however. Here is the paradox: Conspiracy beliefs predict not only support for direct democracy but *also* increased support for autocratic forms of governance where one strong leader makes most of the important policy decisions (Papaioannou et al., 2024). The key explanation for this finding is that conspiracy theories predict a rejection of the political status quo. Conspiracy theories stimulate a political worldview assuming that the current system of representative democracy is rotten to its core; consequently, any alternative would be an improvement, including democratic and undemocratic ones. Indeed, conspiracy beliefs are associated with a desire to burn existing political institutions to the ground and rebuild them from their core (Petersen et al., 2023).

An extreme manifestation of these processes can be found in the *Reichsbürger* movement, a far-right conspiracy movement in Germany. This movement has clear overlap with the sovereign citizen movement, as many citizens do not recognize the rule of law. The movement is also known to reject democracy. In fact, some members within the movement propagate a reintroduction of the monarchy as it existed in 1871. These people believe that constitutional changes after that time (the Weimar republic of 1919; the Federal Republic of Germany after WWII) were illegitimate, and that therefore society should reinstall an Emperor.

In sum, conspiracy beliefs are associated with an increased likelihood of rejecting the rule of law. This may manifest itself in minor rule violations but also in more serious forms of crime. Relatedly, conspiracy beliefs predict a rejection of the system of representative democracy and make both democratic and undemocratic alternatives more appealing. Such a rejection of the rule of law makes extremist action that violate the law, or that target democratic institutions, seem more legitimate.

EXTREMIST VIOLENCE

In far-right extremist groups, a popular conspiracy theory is the so-called "Great Replacement Theory": The belief that a conspiracy exists that seeks to gradually replace the White population of Western nations with immigrants or Muslims. This belief is potentially dangerous. By portraying relatively vulnerable minority groups as a threatening outgroup, this conspiracy theory may legitimize extremist violence against these groups. Indeed, various terrorist attacks in recent history were inspired by variants of the Great Replacement Theory. The 2019 El Paso shooting at Walmart was targeted at the Latino community in Texas. The shooter, Patrick Crucius, had posted a manifesto on 8chan prior to the attack motivating his actions with arguments drawn from the Great Replacement Theory, describing what he saw as a "Hispanic invasion of Texas". A few months earlier, Brenton Tarrant went on a killing spree in two Mosques in Christchurch, New Zealand. He also had posted a manifesto online to justify his actions. The title of his manifesto? "The Great Replacement". And Anders Breivik motivated his killings in Oslo and Utøya (Norway), with "Eurabia" conspiracy theories—which essentially is the Great Replacement Theory applied to Europe. Empirical research supports a link between belief in the Great Replacement Theory with persecution of, and violent intentions towards, Muslims (Obaidi et al., 2022).

Psychological theories designed to explain such violent extremism often highlight grievances as a main driver of radicalization—such as humiliation, losses, inequality, oppression, or other forms of personal or group-based injustice. One impactful theory is Kruglanski's 3N-model of radicalization (Need, Narrative, Network), which stresses that grievances can install a *Need* for significance: A need to matter, and to be respected by valued social groups. This need for significance can lead to extremist violence if such actions are consistent with a terrorism-justifying ideology (i.e., *Narrative*), and supported by a *Network* of valued, like-minded others. Conspiracy theories fit well in these processes. Conspiracy theories provide a narrative demonizing another group, by portraying it as evil and dangerous. Relatedly, conspiracy theories provide a culprit for one's grievances, and clarify which enemy needs to be defeated. As such, conspiracy theories suggest that one's need for significance can be satisfied by turning oneself into a hero who is fighting an important, meaningful, and epic battle with a dangerous enemy (Kruglanski et al., 2022). While conspiracy theories alone are not enough to incite extremist violence, they do seem to facilitate the process of radicalization.

The link between conspiracy beliefs and a propensity for extremist violence can be seen in a variety of ways. One is the methods that people use to protest. Broadly, two forms of collective action can be distinguished. Normative collective action means protesting within the confines of the law—such as peaceful protests, critical blog posts, debating political opponents, or petitions. Non-normative collection means protesting in an illegal and often coercive manner—examples would be violent protests, demolishing property, and harassing or intimidating public figures. This latter form of protest underscores a democratic paradox: A hallmark of democracy is that people are allowed to protest against policy they disagree with; however, the method of protesting that people may choose (e.g., trying to impose one's will on society through violence) is not always democratic. How do conspiracy theories fit into these issues? One study has found that stronger belief in conspiracy theories was associated with a decreased likelihood of engaging in normative (and hence, democratic) forms of protest. Clearly, one does not have to be a conspiracy theorist to disagree with policy and express one's discontent. However, conspiracy beliefs also were associated with an increased likelihood of non-normative (and hence, undemocratic) forms of protest (Imhoff et al., 2021). Presumably, if one believes a government is involved in nefarious conspiracies, one may believe relatively extreme measures are necessary.

Also other studies support a link between belief in conspiracy theories, protest, and a willingness to use violence. In Germany, left-wing hippies marched alongside right-wing Neo-Nazis to jointly (and sometimes violently) protest the lockdowns during the COVID-19 pandemic. A survey fielded in a number of German anti-lockdown Telegram groups indicated that belief in conspiracy theories was one of the factors that united these otherwise different extremist groups and motivated them to protest (Liekefett, Bürner, & Becker, 2023). Another study has found direct evidence for a link between conspiracy mentality and violent extremist intentions. These intentions were measured through questions, for instance assessing if participants were willing to support an organization that fights for their political or legal rights even if it sometimes resorts to violence, or if they would join a protest against oppression of their group that they knew might turn violent (Rottweiler & Gill, 2022). Finally, some studies have found a link between belief in conspiracy theories and a willingness to demolish property (Jolley & Paterson, 2020; Šrol et al., 2022).

All of these studies have relied on quantitative research methods. While these methods are useful to establish meaningful relationships of conspiracy beliefs with a range of relevant variables, they also leave a number of questions about violent extremism unanswered. How prevalent are conspiracy theories among members of extremist fringe groups in society, and to what extent do conspiracy theories inspire violence among their members? Think of underground groups of Neo-Nazis or White supremacists (far-right), anti-globalization extremists or communist revolutionary groups (far-left), and also religious extremist groups such as Al Qaeda, Islamic State, Christian anti-abortion extremists, or cults. Doing research among members of extremist fringe groups using standardized psychological questionnaires is often difficult, as it can be challenging to find enough people willing to participate and acquire a sample size that yields sufficient statistical power.

One can also learn a lot about conspiracy theories using qualitative research methods, however, examining the rhetoric in such groups. One interesting study analyzed over 50 extremist fringe groups in the UK, Europe, and the US by looking if, and to what extent, conspiracy theories were mentioned in their official documents or recorded speeches (Bartlett & Miller, 2010). The study included a host of religious extremist groups, including Al Qaeda, Hamas, Army of God, Lambs of Christ, Jewish extremist groups, and various cults such as "Peoples Temples"; the study also included far-right groups such as Aryan Nations, the Ku Klux Klan, British People's Party, and various right-wing militias; at the far-left the study included groups such as the Angry Brigade, the Red Army Faction, and Anti-Globalization Extremists; and, the study included a few ideologically extreme groups that could not clearly be classified on a political or religious dimension, such as anti-technology groups including the "Committee for Liquidation of Computers" (a violent group that was responsible for attacks on various computer centers in the early 1980s), and revolutionary political groups that combat both communism and capitalism.

Surely such a diverse array of extremist fringe groups cannot have much in common. Or can they? At least one factor seemed to connect most of these groups, which was that their formal documents, and the recorded speeches by their group leaders, contained conspiracy theories. Not every fringe group in this study seemed to extensively use conspiracy theories—for instance, the researchers did not find conspiracy theories in the documents of the "Real IRA". But for the majority of groups under investigation, the researchers observed conspiracy theories in their documentation. There were subtle differences in the conspiracy theories that the groups adhered to, with some groups believing that Jewish conspiracies control world governments (far right), others believing in a Western conspiracy to destroy Islam (e.g., Al Qaeda), and again others in a conspiracy of financiers and bankers to have excessive power over the world (far-left), to name a few. But there were also many resemblances across these groups, such as anti-establishment conspiracy theories, and a frequently recurring belief in a totalitarian world government (e.g., a "New World Order"). As concluded by the authors, "It is striking that there is considerable overlap and fusion between many of these conspiracies, even across groups that exist at opposite ends of the ideological spectrum" (p. 4).

Some of the extremist fringe groups under investigation were violent, and others were not. Was there a difference between violent versus nonviolent fringe groups? These researchers, Jamie Bartlett and Carl Miller, found that conspiracy theories occurred among both the violent and the nonviolent groups. It would therefore be too simple to conclude that conspiracy theories necessarily lead to violence: Although conspiracy theories can sometimes inspire extremist violence such as terrorism, they do not have to. Instead, these authors concluded that conspiracy theories work as a "radicalizing multiplier": Conspiracy theories exacerbate the dynamics underlying extremism, thereby accelerating the process of radicalization. Furthermore, they can contribute to the process through which groups that already are ideologically extreme turn violent. Put differently, conspiracy theories make groups ideologically more extreme, and once this extremism passed a certain threshold, conspiracy theories can contribute to these groups turning violent.

Bartlett and Miller highlight three more specific processes through which conspiracy theories act as a radicalizing multiplier. The first process is much in line with the group processes described in Chapter 4: Conspiracy theories demonize outsiders. Extremist fringe groups make rather sharp distinctions between "us" versus "them", and conspiracy theories enable these groups to solidify a strong identity among its members by fueling aversion against different groups. The second process is that conspiracy theories enable extremist groups to discredit criticism of the group. Dissenting voices may threaten the cohesion of extremist groups, but conspiracy theories enable these groups to portray critics as part of a hostile conspiracy. For instance, journalists may publicly criticize far-right extremist groups; however, these groups may dismiss such criticism through conspiracy theories, for instance by asserting that Jewish conspiracies control the media. And third, conspiracy theories can give extremist fringe groups the feeling that violence is the only remaining option. Conspiracy theories can add to the sense that the group—or the cause that the group stands for—is under imminent attack by a hostile conspiracy, that there is an urgent need for an adequate response, and that a peaceful reaction is unlikely to be effective.

Altogether, both quantitative and qualitative research supports a link between conspiracy beliefs and extremist violence. At the same time, conspiracy theories are not the only factor: Conspiracy theories may contribute to the processes that shape people's willingness to use violence in their pursuit of ideological goals, but there are also many conspiracy theorists who are not violent at all. Moreover, most quantitative research on these issues is still correlational. More evidence is therefore needed to establish the causal paths of the link between conspiracy beliefs and violent extremism. At present it is impossible to conclude with certainty whether belief in conspiracy theories directly causes extremist violence, or rather, whether people merely use conspiracy theories to justify their use of extremist violence afterwards. Both possibilities seem plausible, and they are not mutually exclusive.

CONCLUDING REMARKS

The present chapter has examined the link between conspiracy theories and radicalism on a sliding scale, ranging from regular citizens who have relatively more extreme beliefs than average (e.g., supporting a populist party) or engage in minor forms of civic disobedience (e.g., not respecting physical distancing regulations during the COVID-19 lockdowns), to citizens who are member of terrorist organizations and commit extremist violence. Altogether, the evidence suggests that across this sliding scale, belief in conspiracy theories is associated with radical attitudes and behaviors. Conspiracy beliefs predict populist attitudes and other relatively extreme political beliefs; conspiracy beliefs decrease citizens' willingness obey the law, increase the likelihood that they reject the system of representative democracy, and increase their willingness to accept sometimes undemocratic alternatives (e.g., autocracy); and finally, belief in conspiracy theories predicts an increased support for extremist violence, and conspiracy theories are common in the rhetoric of underground radical groups. By portraying opposing groups as dangerous enemies, conspiracy theories can polarize and radicalize citizens.

6

EXPLAINING AND REDUCING CONSPIRACY THEORIES IN A MODERN WORLD

Each February and March, I am teaching my favorite course of the year: A course on Moral and Political Psychology for the Research Master Social Psychology students at VU Amsterdam. I have developed the course from scratch, and it addresses many of my academic interests including two lectures on conspiracy theories. In 2025, my students had prepared a special surprise for me: As I entered the room, everyone was waiting for me wearing a tinfoil hat! And they had one ready for me as well. Of course, challenge accepted, and I taught the entire lecture wearing a tinfoil hat. It was one of the most memorable, funny, and precious experiences I have had as a teacher. The whole event reminded me of an interview I gave more than 10 years earlier for the local journal "Ad Valvas" of my university. After the interview the journalist asked if I would mind having my picture taken while wearing a tinfoil hat (an incident I had described more elaborately in the first edition of this book). Slightly off-guard I agreed and considered it a good joke at the time—although I might have reconsidered had I known that the picture would end up on the journal's front cover, guided with a quote of me allegedly saying "conspiracy theorists are very sane" (I actually had said that conspiracy theorists do not necessarily have pathologies).

DOI: 10.4324/9781003530718-6

Such tinfoil hats match a common impression of conspiracy theo-rists as socially awkward individuals, who have lost all touch with reality, and believe rather outrageous theories such as that tinfoil hats would protect them from radiation that the government uses to manipulate their mind. Some of the theories discussed in this book indeed are exceptionally bizarre, ranging from alien lizards to chemtrails to flat earth theories. But while such delusional peo-ple do exist, it is important to keep in mind that most people who believe conspiracy theories are not like that. Some conspiracy theo-ries are widespread and are endorsed by large numbers of regular citizens who are doing just fine in their lives—including a good job, a happy family, and a rich social life. These include theories such as that the coronavirus was created in the lab, that pharmaceuti-cal companies hide dangerous side-effects of vaccines, that scien-tists deliberately exaggerate the perils of climate change, and that the press conspires with the government to spread lies about the war in Ukraine. Furthermore, whilst conspiracy theories are slightly more common in the lower educated segment of society, they are by no means exclusive to this segment as they also emerge among high-profile managers, actors, scientists, lawyers, and even power-ful politicians such as the current US President Trump. Conspiracy theories are a common part of public discourse, and we do not need to go online to learn about them as we can also hear them in bars, at parties, on the streets, in public transport, at the grocery store, and so on.

Why are some conspiracy theories so widespread? In this final and concluding chapter, I will first summarize the insights of the previous chapters and draw a series of conclusions. One of the main mistakes that one can make in explaining conspiracy beliefs is to dis-miss them as pathological. Instead, my conclusion will be that con-spiracy theories emerge from regular and predictable psychological processes. After that, I will raise a few suggestions for interventions to reduce the spread of conspiracy theories and focus specifically on social media and the Internet.

WHY ARE CONSPIRACY THEORIES WIDESPREAD?

In our modern world, conspiracy theories mostly proliferate in the online environment. They occur frequently in some closed online communities (such as Telegram groups focused on QAnon, or anti-vaccination groups), on relatively radical message boards or social media platforms (8kun; Parler), but also on mainstream social media platforms that are routinely used by millions of people (X; Facebook). The online environment has numerous features that may facilitate the spread of conspiracy theories. People can easily find support for their conspiracy theories online, enabling them to uphold their conspiracy beliefs via the confirmation bias. People may "infect" each other with conspiracy theories, by spreading links to unreliable conspiratorial content in their social networks. Once people have displayed an interest in conspiracy theories, algorithmic amplification may prioritize conspiratorial content in their newsfeeds. Through a combination of these processes, people may encounter some conspiracy theories quite regularly—and repeated exposure increases the perceived credibility of such content (the "illusory truth effect") (Udry & Barber, 2024).

These insights make it tempting to blame the widespread conspiracy theories in public discourse all on the Internet and social media. I believe that would be too simplistic, however, as it ignores the fact that conspiracy theories were widespread also long before the Internet existed. While the online environment certainly has been a game-changer and is an important factor to consider in the modern world (and a good place to implement interventions), ultimately it is an information and communication medium. One cannot discard psychology to understand conspiracy beliefs. It is still a human choice to believe or disbelieve a particular conspiracy theory. To some extent, people choose what information they wish to be exposed to. They select the information to search for, or the online social networks they wish to be part of, themselves. And when algorithms prioritize conspiratorial content in a user's newsfeed, it is a human choice to click on such content and read it. If one expresses no interest in conspiracy theories, any algorithmic amplification of such content is likely to dissipate quickly and replace it with other content. Technology may contribute to conspiracy beliefs, but only by catering to basic preferences of the human mind.

These considerations underscore that while technological developments certainly matter, psychology is, and always will be, indispensable to understand why many people believe conspiracy theories. Distressed feelings, caused by existentially threatening events or more structural forms of adversity, are a key causal factor to explain why conspiracy theories are prevalent among large segments of the population. These aversive feelings explain why conspiracy theories flourish in the wake of societal crisis situations. This includes both sudden crises such as terrorist strikes, natural disasters, or the unexpected death of a public figure, and ongoing crises such as climate change, epidemics, or wars. In the absence of an unambiguous and objectively real crisis event, negative feelings also can cause conspiracy theories. Uncertainty about the future, feelings of alienation, fast-changing power structures in society, rapid technological advancement, or a deep-rooted distrust towards formal authorities, can all stimulate conspiracy theories. Existential threats elicit sense-making processes in which people assume the worst, increasing people's suspicious feelings towards powerful, dissimilar, or distrusted outgroups. These suspicious feelings can be understood and summarized in terms of the following three complementary insights that follow from Chapters 3, 4, and, 5, and that help explain why conspiracy theories are widespread.

Insight 1: *An intuitive mindset makes people susceptible to conspiracy theories, although people may subsequently maintain and reinforce their conspiracy beliefs through a more deliberative mindset.*

When people experience feelings of existential threat, they are keen on rapidly making sense of their environment. This is a natural, evolved response designed to quickly establish the nature of the threat, enabling a functional response. Correspondingly, conspiracy beliefs originate through a range of intuitive mental processes that allow for such fast sense-making. These processes include the automatic cognitive processes of pattern perception and agency detection; they include the use of heuristics, particularly proportionality and representativeness; and conspiracy beliefs are closely coupled with feelings and emotions. While mostly negative emotions have been associated with conspiracy beliefs, also emotional intensity, and several positive emotions seem to play a role in people's belief in conspiracy theories. This intuitive mindset does not preclude a role for a more deliberate mindset, however, in which people elaborate more carefully about conspiracy theories. Once emotionally invested in the belief that a conspiracy theory must be true, people may engage in the confirmation bias. Much like a lay detective, they use their analytic reasoning skills to find evidence for a conspiracy theory. In doing so, people often selectively embrace evidence that support a conspiracy theory while dismissing or ignoring evidence against it.

All of these sense-making processes underlying belief in conspiracy theories—including those associated with the intuitive mindset that facilitate people to accept conspiracy theories, as well as those associated with a deliberative mindset that help people maintain their conspiracy beliefs—are not pathological; to the contrary, they are perfectly normal. Our minds continuously perform the processes associated with an intuitive mindset, and often these processes are functional to form quick impressions of people or situations. Motivated reasoning is common too. People routinely justify their beliefs, their preferences, and their choices—even when they sometimes may defy logic or reason. One reason why conspiracy theories are widespread among regular citizens, therefore, is because they involve normal and otherwise functional psychological processes.

Insight 2: Conspiracy theories have social roots. They contribute to intergroup conflict by supporting a positive social identity while also demonizing other groups.

Humans are social beings. People have a natural tendency to affiliate with others and have a fundamental need to belong to social groups. Such groups also provide comfort when people feel distressed. Feelings of existential threat increase the extent to which people value their group memberships (Burke et al., 2010). The power of this "need to belong" becomes apparent particularly when people are excluded by others, or by groups that they value—a romantic breakup, a rejection by people previously considered to be friends, or a denial to attend a party that everyone else is invited to. Such social exclusion ranks among the most aversive experiences in life, which undermines self-esteem, and lowers the feeling that one belongs, that one is in control, and that life is meaningful. Social exclusion hurts—in fact, neurological evidence suggests that experiencing exclusion activates the same brain regions as experiencing physical pain (Eisenberger et al., 2003). Why is social exclusion so painful? Because it is in our nature to desire having meaningful social relationships with other people. People have a need to connect themselves selves to valuable others, and to proudly call the resulting collective "We" and "Us".

But when there is a "We", often there is also a "They"—a group of outsiders that is perceived as different from "Us". People continuously categorize their social world into ingroups and outgroups, and their ingroups constitute an important part of their identity. Conspiracy theories increase the salience of such intergroup distinctions, and pit groups against each other. The intuitive mindset described under Insight 1 is in itself not enough to produce conspiracy theories; one also needs to blame their aversive feelings on a group of outsiders. When an outgroup, which is perceived as different or untrustworthy, is salient during times of existential threat, conspiracy theories about that outgroup provide people with a convenient scapegoat to blame their circumstances on.

Chapter 4 has proposed that conspiracy theories polarize groups against each other through two distinct but interrelated paths. The first one is that conspiracy theories contribute to a favorable view of their own group. Conspiracy theories do this via a range of complementary processes. Sometimes, conspiracy theories themselves can become a vital part of people's identity, and form the basis of group memberships (e.g., QAnon). But even when that does not happen, conspiracy theories can help people maintain a positive social identity. By underscoring the moral inferiority of other groups, conspiracy theories enable a perception of one's own group as morally superior. Also, conspiracy theories can deflect status threats. When another group has outperformed one's own group in a competition—which may be a lost election, a lost sports match, or more structural deprivations of status or resources in society—conspiracy theories enable external attributions that helps protect a positive identity. Through conspiracy theories people may believe that the only reason why we lost, or are in this position, is because the other group did not play fair.

Whereas this first path describes the various ways conspiracy theories move people psychologically closer to their own groups, the second path describes how conspiracy theories psychologically push people away from different groups. Conspiracy theories portray a different group as deceptive, harmful, and a liability for the future. By transforming an abstract sense of distrust into a concrete allegation of misconduct, conspiracy theories highlight the suspected dangers of another group. Conspiracy theories may therefore mobilize group members against different groups and ultimately may increase their willingness to fight against this different group.

These social processes underlying conspiracy theories also are not pathological: Conspiracy theories are associated with the basic human tendency to categorize the world into ingroups and outgroups. Moreover, the suspicious feelings that people may have about different groups are not always irrational. The Adaptive Conspiracism Hypothesis has stated that a human propensity to believe conspiracy theories in threatening situations has evolved as a function of millennia of bloody intergroup conflict (Van Prooijen & Van Vugt, 2018). Throughout history groups have turned out dangerous or deceptive and have planned malevolent actions against other groups, ranging from theft to genocide. But people often make mistakes in this process and see conspiracies where there is unlikely to be one. In sum, conspiracy theories have social roots: Feelings of existential threat stimulate conspiracy theories particularly if people can blame the harm they experience on an antagonistic outgroup.

Insight 3: Conspiracy theories are closely associated with radicalism.

These social roots suggest that conspiracy theories can polarize people against others. This is closely coupled with more radical attitudes that include demonization of other groups, and sometimes with radical behavior including violence towards other groups. Relatedly, a well-known insight from the radicalization literature is that feelings of existential threat can stimulate relatively rigid, extreme ideological beliefs. For instance, theories of compensatory conviction state that people compensate for their uncertain feelings in one domain with increased certainty in other domains, most often their ideological beliefs (McGregor, 2006). Also, feelings of social exclusion can make radical groups seem more appealing (Hales & Williams, 2018). Interestingly, these processes are not exclusive to people with low social-economic status. Research on the so-called "wealth paradox" has underscored that people with high social-economic status also can be susceptible to relatively radical ideologies. Wealthy people may have their own sets of anxieties and insecurities, notably the fear of losing their privileges and fall back to a lower status in society (Mols & Jetten, 2017).

Chapter 5 has described that conspiracy theories are associated with a myriad of radical attitudes and behaviors, which may include relatively common forms of radicalism (e.g., voting for a populist leader; supporting a far-right political movement), but also rule violations, undemocratic attitudes, violent forms of protest, and ultimately even membership in underground extremist groups. The relationship between extremism and conspiracy theories is partly connected with the previous insight about intergroup conflict:

Extreme ideologies have a strong tendency to frame the world into a conflict between "Us" versus "Them" (e.g., "Us" the people versus "Them" the corrupt elites). But there is more to it than that. For instance, both radical beliefs and conspiracy theories offer clarity about the causes of societal problems. Instead of appreciating the complexity of societal problems, extremist ideologies provide simple explanations—for instance, by asserting that they are caused deliberately by a conspiracy of corrupt outgroup members.

Whilst radical and extremist ideologies have done much harm in the past century, they are not a result of pathology. Extreme ideologies can emerge when people have strong concerns about societal injustices that they perceive, and when they endorse their moral beliefs with strong conviction. Furthermore, it should be noted that the strong ideological convictions that are part of radicalism have given humanity not only a lot of bad but also a lot of good. Strong ideologies have been responsible for terrorism, oppression, and slavery, but also for important societal change such as increased equality, democracy, and constitutional protection of basic human rights. It was not that long ago when favoring equal rights regardless of race was considered an extremist ideological position (e.g., the civil rights movements in the 1960s). For better or worse, strong ideological beliefs are associated with belief in conspiracy theories, often about groups holding opposite ideological beliefs.

In summary, why are conspiracy theories widespread among normal citizens? Because conspiracy theories are rooted in normal psychological processes. Feelings of existential threat prompt an intuitive mindset that favor simple and compelling explanations for distressing events; such feelings also increase the human tendency to categorize people into "good" ingroups versus "bad" outgroup; and, existential threats increase people's susceptibility to relatively radical ideologies, and their willingness to engage in radical behaviors. Furthermore, actual conspiracies can and do occur, suggesting that not all conspiracy theories are irrational to begin with. Being susceptible to conspiracy theories may be a natural aspect of the human condition.

HOW CAN WE REDUCE BELIEF IN CONSPIRACY THEORIES?

Given the observation that real conspiracies sometimes occur, I feel compelled to start a section on reducing conspiracy theories with a disclaimer: Reducing conspiracy theories is not the same as promoting gullibility among the public. It is also not an attempt to curb efforts to reduce corruption, to suppress dissent among citizens, or to excuse officials who actually commit corruption. Being a good citizen means being a constructively critical citizen, who follows the actions of decision-makers with great interest, and who speak their mind when seeing bad policy or actual integrity violations. But many conspiracy theories are not critical; I'd rather call them cynical. It is not critical, but instead irrational and harmful, to believe that pharmaceutical companies hide evidence that vaccines cause autism. It is also irrational and harmful to believe that climate change is a hoax. The public can contribute to good governance with constructive criticism designed to improve policy, but they also can undermine good governance with cynical conspiracy theories that have no basis in reality and ignore the actual problems that society faces. Reducing conspiracy theories does not mean ignoring actual corruption; it means improving people's capacity to recognize when conspiratorial allegations are implausible.

Researchers have spent a lot of attention in recent years trying to identify psychological interventions to reduce false conspiracy beliefs. Many of these interventions focus on misinformation more broadly and take place in the online environment, as nowadays implausible conspiracy theories mostly spread through social media and the Internet. I should add that also beyond psychology, policymakers have implemented interventions designed to reduce the prevalence and spread of conspiracy theories online. An important example is that the European Union has implemented the Digital

Services Act: A legal framework that compels both VLOPs (Very Large Online Platforms) and VLOSEs (Very Large Online Search Engines) to act against misinformation and false conspiracy theories online. At the time of writing this book, this legal framework is under pressure from the US Trump administration, which considers most forms of content moderation that this framework encourages "censorship".

Psychological interventions to reduce belief in conspiracy theories mostly focus on making people aware of the factual inaccuracies of specific conspiracy theories or making people more resilient against the arguments of conspiracy influencers. To some extent, this seems antithetical to some of the basic insights described earlier of why conspiracy theories are widespread. After all, people accept conspiracy theories mostly through an intuitive mindset and due to social identity concerns, and use rational thought merely to justify, and find evidence for, their conspiracy theories. Noting that particularly intuitive processes and identity concerns drive conspiracy beliefs does not mean that people are willing to entirely abandon reason, logic, or evidence, however. One should again be careful not to make a caricature of people who endorse conspiracy theories. While the "tinfoil hat" types I started this chapter with do exist and are unlikely to be persuaded easily, a much larger group of citizens is unsure what to believe. They may be sensitive to the rhetoric of conspiracy influencers; however, they also may be persuaded by logic, reason, and evidence. These people may be quite susceptible to good arguments, and sensitive to the possibility that they might have been misled.

One problem, however, is that finding accurate information is not always people's main motivation to have an active social media account. Many people are on social media exactly for social identity concerns: To connect with others, to get "likes" for their posts, to get signs of social approval, to get their opinions validated by a receptive audience. In an interesting study, participants were presented with true or false news that was ideologically attractive to either Democrats (e.g., supporting Democrats or disparaging Republicans) or Republicans (e.g., supporting Republicans or disparaging Democrats) (Rathje et al., 2023). In line with people's motivated reasoning tendencies and the social roots described in this book, people were particularly likely to believe false news when it was ideologically attractive, and to disbelieve true news from the opposing party. Half of the participants, however, were incentivized to recognize truth: They would get an additional financial bonus for each news item correctly identified as true or false. This bonus increased participants' performance at this task and decreased their willingness to share false news with others. When participants were motivated to identify news items that their political ingroup would find attractive, however, their performance decreased. Whether people accept false conspiracy theories and misinformation online partly depends on their motivations; and the motivation for truth versus the motivation for a positive social identity do not always align.

Accordingly, researchers have examined the possibility that shifting people's attention away from social identity concerns, and towards the possibility that the information they encounter might be inaccurate, might help in reducing the spread of misinformation and conspiracy theories. One study examined Twitter users who had previously shared links of unreliable, conspiracist websites. The researchers had sent these users a single, non-political headline with the request to assess whether the headline was true or false. This simple intervention—shifting people's attention to the possible accuracy or inaccuracy of the information they encounter—increased the quality of the news that these users shared in the next 24 hours (Pennycook et al., 2021). An intuitive mindset leads people to accept conspiracy theories as true—and, apparently, activating their deliberative mindset therefore increases the likelihood that people reject false conspiracy theories.

Relatedly, research has supported a positive role of so-called warning labels (Martel & Rand, 2023). Social media companies regularly flag content that fact-checkers have identified as unreliable or false. This policy might be seen as a compromise between removing unreliable content entirely versus allowing all ideas (no matter how wrong and harmful) to be ventilated without restrictions. Such warning labels shift users to the possible inaccuracy of information before they share it in their personal networks. It should be noted, however, that some warning labels work better than others. For instance, warning labels work best if they are clearly visible, and if they are specific and precise in clarifying what exact information is false. If warning labels are too general—for instance alerting people to the possibility that some information they will encounter might be false, without further clarification—the risk is that people also may be more likely to judge true information as false. Warning labels are hence a promising intervention (and encouraged by the EU Digital Services Act) but need to be implemented carefully.

Shifting participants mindset from intuitive to deliberative (by shifting people's attention to the possibility that the information they read might be false) hence seems to be a useful tool in combating conspiracy theories and misinformation online. These interventions, however, only focus on people's acceptance of conspiracy theories when they encounter them. Other interventions have focused on making people more resilient to conspiracy theories before they encounter them (prebunking) or on rationally refuting conspiracy theories (debunking), thus attempting to reduce belief in conspiracy theories after having accepted them as true.

Prebunking

Prebunking has analogies with inoculation in the context of disease prevention: By vaccinating people with a small dose of a virus, people develop immunity against it. Likewise, providing people with small bits of misinformation or false conspiracy theories can help them develop counterarguments, and may increase their resilience against such misleading information. Prebunking hence is designed to bolster people's critical mindset towards conspiracy theories before being exposed to them. Prebunking can take place in the context of one specific conspiracy theory: For instance, people may learn arguments why a particular conspiracy theory is invalid before they are exposed to influencers arguing for the theory. Such prebunking of specific theories is limited in practice, as it is not always easy to predict what conspiracy theories will become popular, and through social media a new conspiracy theory can spread quickly. Prebunking also can be more general, however, and pertains to teaching people how to recognize false conspiracy theories and misinformation more broadly. Such general prebunking includes highlighting what the characteristic features are of most false news items, recognizing some of the manipulative rhetorical tricks that conspiracy influencers use, and emphasizing what sources produce unreliable content.

Overall, research has found promising effects of prebunking on people's belief in misinformation and false conspiracy theories (Van der Linden, 2022). Also, the Dutch psychologist Sander van der Linden (Cambridge University) has developed useful apps to train people's prebunking skills in a fun, playful manner. There is one drawback to prebunking, however, which is that its effects wear off over time. Much like an actual vaccine, sometimes a "booster" shot may be necessary to keep people's skills to think critically about conspiracy theories in shape.

These considerations suggest that more research is necessary on the question what may improve the likelihood that prebunking interventions "stick" over time. One possibility that future research might explore is teaching prebunking skills as part of broader social media literacy courses in high school curricula. While the possible benefits of such an intervention for long-term resilience against conspiracy theories are speculative at this point, in general it is the case that skills that people learn at a younger age are more likely to last over time. Moreover, some adolescents spend many hours a week online and may be poorly prepared for the conspiratorial rhetoric they might encounter, as well as other hateful, extremist content (e.g., the Incel-movement, which spreads hateful content about women among young men). Making young people resilient against conspiracy theories, as well as related issues such as misinformation and hate speech, seems to be an important challenge in a digital world.

Debunking

While prebunking focuses on preventing people from becoming "infected" with conspiracy theories, debunking focuses on "curing" people who believe in far-fetched, implausible conspiracy theories. The essence of prebunking is to reduce people's belief in a conspiracy theory by providing rational arguments against it. Through information of fact-checkers and scientific research, and by showing undeniable falsehoods in conspiracy theories, people might change their minds and stop believing in them. One challenge that debunking faces is the confirmation bias, described in Chapter 3. Not everyone is willing to be persuaded, and sometimes people are heavily invested in a conspiracy theory. Still, overall debunking appears to have a small but positive effect, underscoring that not all people who believe conspiracy theories are immune to reason and evidence.

A common concern that is often raised against debunking is the risk of so-called "backfire effects": The possibility that debunking efforts make people only more invested in a particular conspiracy theory. For instance, people might interpret a debunking intervention as a further attempt by a conspiracy to mislead them, thus reinforcing existing conspiratorial beliefs. While such backfire effects have been found occasionally, overall, this concern seems unwarranted. Backfire effects, if they occur, are relatively rare; far more common is that debunking interventions contribute to a small but significant reduction in conspiracy beliefs (Nyhan, 2021).

Quite interesting is the notion that Artificial Intelligence (AI) might play a role in reducing conspiracy theories through debunking. AI is often seen as a liability in the context of misinformation and conspiracy theories. For example, deepfakes are increasingly difficult to distinguish from real video materials and are effective in polarizing people (Nieweglowska et al., 2023). Moreover, many people have conspiracy theories about AI itself, for instance asserting that powerholders will abuse AI by violating people's privacy, or that AI itself will conspire to ultimately oppress humanity (as in movies such as "I, Robot" or "The Matrix") (Zhao et al., 2025). An interesting experiment by Thomas Costello and colleagues, however, shows that AI also can be used in a constructive manner to reduce conspiracy theories. Participants first described a conspiracy theory in which they believed, and then discussed the theory in three rounds with an AI app. In a control condition, participants discussed a neutral topic with the AI app. The discussion with AI reduced participants' conspiracy beliefs with about 20%; moreover, this reduction was still visible in a follow-up measurement two months later (Costello et al., 2024).

While no research has yet compared the effectiveness of debunking by an AI app versus by humans directly, my impression is that AI is quite effective at debunking—in all likelihood, more so than most humans. Why is AI so good at this? One plausible explanation (also the one favored by the study authors) is that debunking by AI is more compelling, as AI has access to the expert knowledge required to make a persuasive case. For example, imagine debating a person who believes that pharmaceutical companies hide undisclosed side-effects of vaccines. For most people that would be a difficult discussion, as they are not experts on vaccines themselves. They must rely only on superficial knowledge of how vaccines work and how they are tested, and are unprepared for the avalanche of arguments that their conversation partner fires at them. Most people therefore would struggle to identify the mistakes in a conspiracy theorists' reasoning. This lack of expert knowledge also would make it unlikely that the conspiracy theorist takes their conversation partner seriously. But AI does have the required expert knowledge available and can more easily point out what arguments in a conspiracy theorists' line of reasoning are correct and incorrect, and why.

But I suspect more possible processes contribute to this effectiveness of AI. For example, AI apps stay remarkably polite in their conversations with users (certainly more so than many humans who debate a conspiracy theorist) and are unlikely to implicitly or explicitly express signs of contempt. Moreover, people may be less concerned about "saving face" when discussing their conspiracy beliefs with an AI app than with a human being, which might reduce their likelihood of becoming defensive about their beliefs. All these possibilities require further testing. For now, it seems that debunking is a promising intervention to reduce conspiracy beliefs—particularly if AI does it.

IN CLOSING

Conspiracy theories are not endemic to our modern era—they have occurred throughout human history. People have always experienced uncertainty and fear in response to possible danger, and as a means of effectively coping with these aversive feelings, people become vigilant to the possible conspiratorial activities of powerful, and possibly hostile other groups. Such vigilance is not pathological: It is a natural defense mechanism that involves regular psychological processes. But recognizing the basic psychological roots of belief in conspiracy theories does not mean that specific features of the modern digital world are irrelevant for such beliefs. Technological developments of the past few decades—particularly social media and the Internet—have changed human interactions dramatically, and many features of the online environment have introduced new dynamics that are relevant for people's belief in conspiracy theories, and their spread. Online it has become easier than ever to connect with people who have the same beliefs, to spread conspiracy theories to a receptive audience, to mislead people for political purposes, or to find validation of misguided ideas.

Conspiracy theories therefore are common and will continue to be in the foreseeable future. The fact that some conspiracy theories are common do not make them true or rational, however, and it is of utmost importance that scientists continue to work on developing interventions that increase people's resilience to conspiracy theories and prevent their spread. At present the world is facing serious challenges that require responsible solutions, but that are also frequent targets of conspiracy theories—including populism, climate change, war, public health, poverty, discrimination, and unemployment. I therefore hope that the insights about the psychology of conspiracy theories that are offered here may contribute to a more rational society.

FURTHER READING

ACADEMIC OVERVIEW ARTICLES AND META-ANALYSES

Biddlestone, M., Green, R., Douglas, K. M., Azevedo, F., Sutton, R. M., & Cichocka, A. (2025). Reasons to believe: A systematic review and meta-analytic synthesis of the motives associated with conspiracy beliefs. *Psychological Bulletin, 151,* 48–87. https://doi.org/10.1037/bul0000463

Bowes, S. M., Costello, T. H., & Tasimi, A. (2023). The conspiratorial mind: A meta-analytic review of motivational and personological correlates. *Psychological Bulletin, 149,* 259–293. https://doi.org/10.1037/bul0000392

Douglas, K. M., & Sutton, R. M. (2025). The social psychology of conspiracy theories: Key insights and future challenges. *Advances in Experimental Social Psychology, 71,* 1–68. https://doi.org/10.1016/bs.aesp.2024.10.004

Hornsey, M. J., Bierwiaczonek, K., Sassenberg, K., & Douglas, K. M. (2023). Individual, intergroup and nation-level influences on belief in conspiracy theories. *Nature Reviews Psychology, 2,* 85–97. https://doi.org/10.1038/s44159-022-00133-0

Van der Linden, S. (2022). Misinformation: Susceptibility, spread, and interventions to immunize the public. *Nature Medicine, 28,* 460–467. https://doi.org/10.1038/s41591-022-01713-6

Van Prooijen, J.-W. (2024). Group-oriented motivations underlying conspiracy theories. *Group Processes & Intergroup Relations, 27,* 1050–1067. https://doi.org/10.1177/13684302241240696

Van Prooijen, J.-W. Šrol, J., & Maglić, M. (2025). How belief in conspiracy theories could harm sustainability. *Nature Human Behaviour*. https://doi.org/10 .1038/s41562-025-02243-0

EDITED BOOKS AND SPECIAL ISSUES

Butter, M., & Knight, P. (2020). *Routledge handbook of conspiracy theories*. Routledge.

Forgas, J. P. (Ed.). (2025). *The psychology of false beliefs: Cognitive delusions and conspiracy theories*. Routledge.

Miller, M. K. (Ed.). (2025). *The social science of QAnon*. Cambridge University Press.

Sassenberg, K., Bertin, P., Douglas, K. M., & Hornsey, M. (Eds.). (2023). Engaging with conspiracy theories: Causes and consequences. *Journal of Experimental Social Psychology (Special issue)*, 105, 104425.

Uscinski, J. E. (Ed.). (2019). *Conspiracy theories and the people who believe them*. Oxford University Press.

Van Prooijen, J.-W., & Imhoff, R. (Eds.). (2023). Conspiracy theories. *Current Opinion in Psychology (Special issue)*, 48, 101465.

BOOKS FOR A GENERAL AUDIENCE

Butter, M. (2020). *The nature of conspiracy theories*. Polity Press.

DiResta, R. (2024). *Invisible rulers: The people who turn lies into reality*. PublicAffairs.

Merlan, A. (2020). *Republic of lies: American conspiracy theories and their surprising rise to power*. Penguin.

Neiwert, D. (2020). *Red pill, blue pill: How to counteract the conspiracy theories that are killing us*. Prometheus Books.

Shermer, M. (2024). *Conspiracy: Why the rational believe the irrational*. JHU Press.

Van der Linden, S. (2023). *Foolproof: Why misinformation infects our minds and how to build immunity*. W. W. Norton & Co.

Van Prooijen, J.-W. (2024). *Hoax: Waarom mensen in complottheorieën geloven*. A. W. Bruna. (In Dutch; English translation in preparation).

REFERENCES

Abadi, D., Van Prooijen, J.-W., Krouwel, A. P. M., & Fischer, A. (2024). Anti-establishment sentiments: Various types of realistic and symbolic threats predict populist attitudes and conspiracy mentality. *Cognition and Emotion, 38,* 1246–1260. https://doi.org/10.1080/02699931.2024.2360584

Abalakina-Paap, M., Stephan, W. G., Craig, T., & Gregory, W. L. (1999). Beliefs in conspiracies. *Political Psychology, 20*(3), 637–647. https://doi.org/10.1111/0162-895X.00160

Adam-Troian, J., Chayinska, M., Paladino, M. P., Ulug, O. M., Vaes, J., & Wagner-Egger, P. (2023). Of precarity and conspiracy: Introducing a socio-functional model of conspiracy beliefs. *British Journal of Social Psychology, 62,* 136–159. https://doi.org/10.1111/bjso.12597

AIVD (2023). *Anti-institutioneel extremisme in Nederland: Een ernstige bedreiging voor de democratische rechtsorde?* Publicatie Algemene Inlichtingen- en Veiligheidsdienst.

Bartlett, J., & Miller, C. (2010). *The power of unreason: Conspiracy theories, extremism and counter-terrorism.* Demos.

Bertin, P., Delouvée, S., McColl, K., & Van Prooijen, J.-W. (2023). Rage against the machine: Investigating conspiracy theories about the Video Assistant Referee on Twitter during the 2018 FIFA World Cup. *Sports Management Review, 4,* 495–516. https://doi.org/10.1080/14413523.2022.2127179

Bowes, S. M., Costello, T. H., & Tasimi, A. (2023). The conspiratorial mind: A meta-analytic review of motivational and personological correlates. *Psychological Bulletin, 149,* 259–293. https://doi.org/10.1037/bul0000392

Burke, B. L., Martens, A., & Faucher, E. H. (2010). Two decades of terror management theory: A meta-analysis of mortality salience research.

Personality and Social Psychology Review, 14, 155–195. https://doi.org/10.1177/1088868309352321

Butter, M. (2020). *The nature of conspiracy theories*. Polity press.

Costello, T. H., Pennycook, G., & Rand, D. G. (2024). Durably reducing conspiracy theories through dialogues with AI. *Science*, 385, eadq1814. https://doi.org/10.1126/science.adq1814

Crocker, J., Luhtanen, R., Broadnax, S., & Blaine, B. E. (1999). Belief in U.S. government conspiracies against blacks among black and white college students: Powerlessness or system blame? *Personality and Social Psychology Bulletin*, 25, 941–953. https://doi.org/10.1177/01461672992511003

Douglas, K. M., Cichocka, A., & Sutton, R. M. (2017). The psychology of conspiracy theories. *Current Directions in Psychological Science*, 26, 538–542. https://doi.org/10.1177/0963721417718261

Douglas, K. M., & Sutton, R. M. (2023). What are conspiracy theories? A definitional approach to their correlates, consequences, and communication. *Annual Review of Psychology*, 74, 271–298. https://doi.org/10.1146/annurev-psych-032420-031329

Douglas, K. M., Sutton, R. M., Callan, M. J., Dawtry, R. J., & Harvey, A. J. (2016). Someone is pulling the strings: Hypersensitive agency detection and belief in conspiracy theories. *Thinking and Reasoning*, 22, 57–77. https://doi.org/10.1080/13546783.2015.1051586

Eisenberger, N. I., Lieberman, M. D., & Williams, K. D. (2003). Does rejection hurt? A fMRI study of social exclusion. *Science*, 302, 290–292. https://doi.org/10.1126/science.1089134

Epley, N., & Gilovich, T. (2016). The mechanics of motivated reasoning. *Journal of Economic Perspectives*, 30, 133–140. https://doi.org/10.1257/jep.30.3.133

Erisen, C., Guidi, M., Martini, M., Toprakkiran, S., Isernia, P., & Littvay, L. (2021). Psychological correlates of populist attitudes. *Advances in Political Psychology*, 42, 149–172. https://doi.org/10.1111/pops.12768

Federico, C. M. (2022). The complex relationship between conspiracy beliefs and the politics of social change. *Current Opinion in Psychology*, 47, 101354. https://doi.org/10.1016/j.copsyc.2022.101354

Festinger, F. (1957). *A theory of cognitive dissonance*. Stanford University Press.

Fiebig, V., & Koehler, D. (2022). Uncharted territory: Towards an evidence-based criminology of sovereign citizens through a systematic literature review. *Perspectives on Terrorism*, 16, 34–48. https://www.jstor.org/stable/27185090

Gagliardi, L. (2025). The role of cognitive biases in conspiracy beliefs: A literature review. *Journal of Economic Surveys*, 39, 32–65. https://doi.org/10.1111/joes.12604

Golec de Zavala, A., Dyduch-Hazar, K., & Lantos, D. (2019). Collective narcissism: Political consequences of investing self-worth in the ingroup's image. *Advances in Political Psychology*, 40, 37–74. https://doi.org/10.1111/pops.12569

Golec de Zavala, A., & Federico, C. M. (2018). Collective narcissism and the growth of conspiracy thinking over the course of the 2016 United States presidential election: A longitudinal analysis. *European Journal of Social Psychology*, 48, 1011–1018. https://doi.org/10.1002/ejsp.2496

Hales, A. H., & Williams, K. D. (2018). Marginalized individuals and extremism: The role of ostracism in openness to extreme groups. *Journal of Social Issues*, 74, 75–92. https://doi.org/10.1111/josi.12257

Haselton, M. G., & Buss, D. M. (2000). Error management theory: A new perspective on biases in cross-sex mind reading. *Journal of Personality and Social Psychology*, 78, 81–91. https://doi.org/10.1037//0022-3514.78.1.81

Hornsey, M. J., Harris, E. A., & Fielding, K. S. (2018). The psychological roots of anti-vaccination attitudes: A 24-nation investigation. *Health Psychology*, 37, 307–315. https://doi.org/10.1037/hea0000586

Hornsey, M. J., Pearson, S., Kang, J., Sassenberg, K., Jetten, J., Van Lange, P. A. M., ... Bastian, B. (2023). Multination data show that conspiracy beliefs are associated with the perception (and reality) of poor national economic performance. *European Journal of Social Psychology*, 53, 78–89. https://doi.org/10.1002/ejsp.2888

Imhoff, R., Bertlich, T., & Frenken, M. (2022). Tearing apart the "evil" twins: A general conspiracy mentality is not the same as specific conspiracy beliefs. *Current Opinion in Psychology*, 46, Article 101349. https://doi.org/10.1016/j.copsyc.2022.101349

Imhoff, R., & Bruder, M. (2014). Speaking (un-)truth to power: Conspiracy mentality as a generalized political attitude. *European Journal of Personality*, 28, 25–43. https://doi.org/10.1002/per.1930

Imhoff, R., Dieterle, L., & Lamberty, P. (2021). Resolving the puzzle of conspiracy worldview and political activism: Belief in secret plots decreases normative but increases nonnormative political engagement. *Social Psychological and Personality Science*, 12, 71–79. https://doi.org/10.1177/1948550619896491

Imhoff, R., & Lamberty, P. (2020). A bioweapon or a hoax? The link between distinct conspiracy beliefs about the coronavirus disease (COVID-19) outbreak and pandemic behavior. *Social Psychological and Personality Science*, 11, 1110–1118. https://doi.org/10.1177/1948550620934692

Imhoff, R., Zimmer, F., Klein, O., António, J. H. C., Babinska, M., Bangerter, A., ... Van Prooijen, J.-W. (2022). Conspiracy mentality and political orientation across 26 countries. *Nature Human Behaviour*, 6, 392–403. https://doi.org/10.1038/s41562-021-01258-7

Jetten, J., Peters, K., & Casara, B. G. S. (2022). Economic inequality and conspiracy theories. *Current Opinion in Psychology*, 47, 101358. https://doi.org/10.1016/j.copsyc.2022.101358

Jolley, D., Douglas, K. M., Leite, A. C., & Schrader, T. (2019). Belief in conspiracy theories and intentions to engage in everyday crime. *British Journal of Psychology*, 58, 534–549. https://doi.org/10.1111/bjso.12311

Jolley, D., Meleady, R., & Douglas, K. M. (2020). Exposure to conspiracy theories promotes prejudice which spreads across groups. *British Journal of Psychology*, 111, 17–35. https://doi.org/10.1111/bjop.12385

Jolley, D., & Paterson, J. L. (2020). Pylons ablaze: Examining the role of 5G COVID-19 conspiracy beliefs and support for violence. *British Journal of Social Psychology*, 59, 628–640. https://doi.org/10.1111/bjso.12394

Kay, A. C., Gaucher, D., McGregor, I., & Nash, K. (2010). Religious conviction as compensatory control. *Personality and Social Psychology Review*, 14, 37–48. https://doi.org/10.1177/1088868309353750

Kim, S., Stavrova, O., & Vohs, K. D. (2022). Do voting and election outcomes predict changes in conspiracy beliefs? Evidence from two high-profile US elections. *Journal of Experimental Social Psychology*, 104396. https://doi.org/10.1016/j.jesp.2022.104396

Kofta, M., Soral, W., & Bilewicz, M. (2020). What breeds conspiracy antisemitism? The role of political uncontrollability and uncertainty in the belief in Jewish conspiracy. *Journal of Personality and Social Psychology*, 118, 900–918. https://doi.org/10.1037/pspa0000183

Krouwel, A., Kutiyski, Y., Van Prooijen, J.-W., Martinsson, J., & Markstedt, E. (2017). Does extreme political ideology predict conspiracy beliefs, economic evaluations and political trust? Evidence from Sweden. *Journal of Social and Political Psychology*, 5, 435–462. https://doi.org/10.5964/jspp.v5i2.745

Kruglanski, A. W., Molinario, E., Ellenberg, M., & Di Cicco, G. (2022). Terrorism and conspiracy theories: A view from the 3N model of radicalization. *Current Opinion in Psychology*, 47, 101396. https://doi.org/10.1016/j.copsyc.2022.101396

LeBoeuf, R. A., & Norton, M. I. (2012). Consequence-cause matching: Looking to the consequences of events to infer their causes. *Journal of Consumer Research*, 39, 128–141. https://doi.org/10.1086/662372

Lewandowsky, S., Lloyd, E. A., & Brophy, S. (2020). When THUNCing trumps thinking: What distant alternative worlds can tell us about the real world. *Argumenta*, 3, 217–231. https://doi.org/10.23811/52.arg2017.lew.llo.bro

Liekefett, L., Bürner, A.-K., & Becker, J. C. (2023). Hippies next to right-wing extremists? Identifying subgroups of antilockdown protesters in Germany using latent profile analysis. *Social Psychology*, 54, 123–135. https://doi.org/10.1027/1864-9335/a000509

Liekefett, L., Christ, O., & Becker, J. C. (2023). Can conspiracy beliefs be beneficial? Longitudinal linkages between conspiracy beliefs, anxiety, uncertainty aversion, and existential threat. *Personality and Social Psychology Bulletin*, 49, 167–179. https://doi.org/10.1177/01461672211060965

Loomba, S., de Figueiredo, A., Piatek, S. J., de Graaf, K., & Larson, H. J. (2021). Measuring the impact of COVID-19 vaccine misinformation on vaccination intent in the UK and USA. *Nature Human Behaviour, 5*, 337–348. https://doi.org /10.1038/s41562-021-01056-1

Mao, J., Van Prooijen, J.-W., & Van Lange, P. A. M. (2024). Conspiracy theories: Groups, ideology, and status as three distinct bases for expressions in society. *Current Directions in Psychological Science, 33*, 385–391. https://doi.org/10.1177 /09637214241280742

Mao, J.-Y., Zeng, Z.-X., Yang, S.-L., Guo, Y.-Y., & Van Prooijen, J.-W. (2023). Explaining the paradox of conspiracy theories and system justifying beliefs from an intergroup perspective. *Political Psychology.* https://doi.org/10.1111/ pops.12924

Martel, C., & Rand, D. (2023). Misinformation warning labels are widely effective: A review of warning effects and their moderating features. *Current Opinion in Psychology, 54*, 101710. https://doi.org/10.1016/j.copsyc.2023.101710

Mashuri, A., & Zaduqisti, E. (2015). The effect of intergroup threat and social identity salience on the belief in conspiracy theories over terrorism in Indonesia: Collective angst as a mediator. *International Journal of Psychological Research, 8*, 24–35. https://doi.org/10.21500/20112084.642

McGregor, I. (2006). Offensive defensiveness: Toward an integrative neuroscience of compensatory zeal after mortality salience, personal uncertainty, and other poignant self-threats. *Psychological Inquiry, 17*, 299–308. https://doi.org/10.1080/10478400701366977

Miller, J. M., Saunders, K. L., & Farhart, C. E. (2016). Conspiracy endorsement as motivated reasoning: The moderating roles of political knowledge and trust. *American Journal of Political Science, 60*(4), 824–844. https://doi.org/10.1111 /ajps.12234

Milli, S., Carroll, M., Pandey, S., Wang, Y., & Dragan, A. D. (2023). Twitter's algorithm: Amplifying anger, animosity, and affective polarization. *ArXiv, abs/2305.16941.* https://doi.org/10.48550/arXiv.2305.16941

Mols, F., & Jetten, J. (2017). *The wealth paradox: Economic prosperity and the hardening of attitudes.* Cambridge University Press.

Mudde, C. (2004). The populist zeitgeist. *Government and Opposition, 39*, 541–563. https://doi.org/10.1111/j.1477-7053.2004.00135.x

Müller, J.-W. (2016). *What is populism?* University of Pennsylvania Press.

Nera, K., Wagner-Egger, P., Bertin, P., Douglas, K. M., & Klein, O. (2021). A power-challenging theory of society, or a conservative mindset? Upward and downward conspiracy theories as ideologically distinct beliefs. *European Journal of Social Psychology, 51*, 740–757. https://doi.org/10.1002/ejsp.2769

Nieweglowska, M., Stellato, C., & Sloman, S. A. (2023). Deepfakes: Vehicles for radicalization, not persuasion. *Current Directions in Psychological Science, 32*, 236–241. https://doi.org/10.1177/09637214231161321

Nyhan, B. (2021). Why the backfire effect does not explain the durability of political misperceptions. *Proceedings of the National Academy of Sciences, 118*, e1912440117. https://doi.org/10.1073/pnas.1912440117

Obaidi, M., Kunst, J., Ozer, S., & Kimel, S. Y. (2022). The "Great Replacement" conspiracy: How the perceived ousting of Whites can evoke violent extremism and Islamophobia. *Group Processes & Intergroup Relations, 25*, 1675–1695. https://doi.org/10.1177/13684302211028293

Oliver, J. E., & Wood, T. (2014). Medical conspiracy theories and health behaviors in the United States. *JAMA Internal Medicine, 174*, 817–818. https://doi.org/10.1001/jamainternmed.2014.190

Pantazi, M., Gkinopoulos, T., Witkowska, M., Klein, O., & Bilewicz, M. (2022). "Historia est magistra vitae"? The impact of historical victimhood on current conspiracy beliefs. *Group Processes & Intergroup Relations, 25*, 581–601. https://doi.org/10.1177/1368430220968898

Pantazi, M., Papaioannou, K., & Van Prooijen, J.-W. (2022). Power to the people: The hidden link between support for direct democracy and belief in conspiracy theories. *Political Psychology, 43*, 529–548. https://doi.org/10.1111/pops.12779

Papaioannou, K., Pantazi, M., & Van Prooijen, J.-W. (2023). Unravelling the relationship between populism and belief in conspiracy theories: The role of cynicism, powerlessness, and zero-sum thinking. *British Journal of Psychology, 114*, 159–175. https://doi.org/10.1111/bjop.12602

Papaioannou, K., Pantazi, M., & Van Prooijen, J.-W. (2024). Rejection of the status quo: Conspiracy theories and preference for alternative political systems. *British Journal of Social Psychology, 63*, 2077–2099. https://doi.org/10.1111/bjso.12754

Pennycook, G., Epstein, Z., Mosleh, M., Arechar, A. A., Eckles, D., & Rand, D. G. (2021). Shifting attention to accuracy can reduce misinformation online. *Nature, 592*, 590–595. https://doi.org/10.1038/s41586-021-03344-2

Petersen, M. B., Osmundsen, M., & Arceneaux, K. (2023). The "need for chaos" and motivations to share hostile political rumors. *American Political Science Review, 117*, 1486–1505. https://doi.org/10.1017/S0003055422001447

Pipes, D. (1997). *Conspiracy: How the paranoid style flourishes and where it comes from.* Simon & Schusters.

Poon, K. T., Chen, Z., & Wong, W. Y. (2020). Beliefs in conspiracy theories following ostracism. *Personality and Social Psychology Bulletin, 46*(8), 1234–1246. https://doi.org/10.1177/0146167219898944

Rathje, J. (2022). Driven by conspiracies: The justification of violence among "Reichsbürger" and other conspiracy-ideological sovereignists in contemporary Germany. *Perspectives on Terrorism, 16*, 49–61. https://www.jstor.org/stable/27185091

Rathje, S., Roozenbeek, J., Van Bavel, J. J., & Van der Linden, S. (2023). Accuracy and social motivations shape judgements of (mis)information. *Nature Human Behaviour*, 7, 892–903. https://doi.org/10.1038/s41562-023-01540-w

Rottweiler, B., & Gill, P. (2022). Conspiracy beliefs and violent extremist intentions: The contingent effects of self-efficacy, self-control and law-related morality. *Terrorism and Political Violence*, 34(7), 1485–1504. https://doi.org/10.1080/09546553.2020.1803288

Schlette, A., Van Prooijen, J.-W., Blokland, A., & Thijs, F. (2023). Information, identity, and action: The messages of the Dutch anti-vaccination community on Telegram. *New Media & Society*. https://doi.org/10.1177/14614448231215735

Skinner, B. F. (1948). 'Superstition' in the pigeon. *Journal of Experimental Psychology*, 38, 168–172. https://doi.org/10.1037/h0055873

Skitka, L. J. (2010). The psychology of moral conviction. *Social and Personality Psychology Compass*, 4, 267–281. https://doi.org/10.1111/j.1751-9004.2010.00254.x

Slovic, P., Finucane, M. L., Peters, E., & MacGregor, D. G. (2007). The affect heuristic. *European Journal of Operational Research*, 177, 1333–1352. https://doi.org/10.1016/j.ejor.2005.04.006

Smallpage, S. M., Enders, A. M., & Uscinksi, J. E. (2017). The partisan contours of conspiracy theory beliefs. *Research and Politics*, 4(4). https://doi.org/10.1177/2053168017746554

Šrol, J., & Čavojová V. (2024). Symbolic threat from the West, belief in pro-Kremlin conspiracy theories, and attribution of blame for the war in Ukraine: A two-wave longitudinal study. *Political Psychology*. https://doi.org/10.1111/pops.12975

Šrol, J., Čavojová V., & Ballová Mikušková, E. (2022). Finding someone to blame: The link between COVID-19 conspiracy beliefs, prejudice, support for violence, and other negative social outcomes. *Frontiers in Psychology*, 12, e726076. https://doi.org/10.3389/fpsyg.2021.726076

Stall, L. M., & Petrocelli, J. V. (2023). Countering conspiracy theory beliefs: Understanding the conjunction fallacy and considering disconfirming evidence. *Applied Cognitive Psychology*, 37, 266–276. https://doi.org/10.1002/acp.3998

Sternisko, A., Cichocka, A., Cislak, A., & Van Bavel, J. J. (2023). National narcissism predicts the belief and dissemination of conspiracy theories during the COVID-19 pandemic: Evidence from 56 countries. *Personality and Social Psychology Bulletin*, 49, 48–65. https://doi.org/10.1177/01461672211054947

Sternisko, A., Delouvée, S., & Van Bavel, J. J. (2022). Clarifying the relationship between randomness dismissal and conspiracist ideation: A preregistered replication and meta-analysis. *Journal of Experimental Social Psychology*, 102, 104357. https://doi.org/10.1016/j.jesp.2022.104357

Swami, V. (2012). Social psychological origins of conspiracy theories: The case of the Jewish conspiracy theory in Malaysia. *Frontiers in Psychology*, 3, 1–9. https://doi.org/10.3389/fpsyg.2012.00280

Symaniak, K., Zajenkowski, M., Fronczyk, K., Leung, S., & Harmon-Jones, E. (2023). Trait anger and approach motivation are related to higher endorsement of specific and generic conspiracy beliefs. *Journal of Research in Personality*, 104, 104374. https://doi.org/10.1016/j.jrp.2023.104374

Thorburn, S., & Bogart, L. M. (2005). Conspiracy beliefs about birth control: Barriers to pregnancy prevention among African Americans of reproductive age. *Health Education & Behavior*, 32, 474–487. https://doi.org/10.1177/1090198105276220

Tingley, D., & Wagner, G. (2017). Solar geoengineering and the chemtrails conspiracy on social media. *Palgrave Communications*, 3, 12. https://doi.org/10.1057/s41599-017-0014-3

Udry, J., & Barber, S. J. (2024). The illusory truth effect: A review of how repetition increases belief in misinformation. *Current Opinion in Psychology*, 56, 101736. https://doi.org/10.1016/j.copsyc.2023.101736.

Uscinski, J., Enders, A., Klofstad, C., Seelig, M., Drochon, H., Premaratne, K., & Muhrti, M. (2022). Have beliefs in conspiracy theories increased over time? *PLoS One*, 17(7), e0270429. https://doi.org/10.1371/journal.pone.0270429

Uscinski, J. E., & Parent, J. M. (2014). *American conspiracy theories*. Oxford University Press.

Van der Linden, S. (2022). Misinformation: Susceptibility, spread, and interventions to immunize the public. *Nature Medicine*, 28, 460–467. https://doi.org/10.1038/s41591-022-01713-6

Van der Linden, S., Panagopoulos, C., Azevedo, F., & Jost, J. J. (2021). The paranoid style in American politics revisited: An ideological asymmetry in conspiratorial thinking. *Political Psychology*, 42, 23–51. https://doi.org/10.1111/pops.12681

Van Elk, M. (2013). Paranormal believers are more prone to illusory agency detection than skeptics. *Consciousness and Cognition*, 22, 1041–1046. https://doi.org/10.1016/j.concog.2013.07.004

Van Prooijen, J.-W. (2017). Why education predicts decreased belief in conspiracy theories. *Applied Cognitive Psychology*, 31, 50–58. https://doi.org/10.1002/acp.3301

Van Prooijen, J.-W. (2019). Belief in conspiracy theories: Gullibility or rational skepticism? In J. P. Forgas & R. F. Baumeister (Eds.), *Homo Credulus: The social psychology of gullibility* (pp. 319–332). Routledge.

Van Prooijen, J.-W. (2020). An existential threat model of conspiracy theories. *European Psychologist*, 25, 16–25. https://doi.org/10.1027/1016-9040/a000381

Van Prooijen, J.-W. (2022). Injustice without evidence: The unique role of conspiracy theories in social justice research. *Social Justice Research*, 35, 88–106. https://doi.org/10.1007/s11211-021-00376-x

Van Prooijen, J.-W. (2024). Group-oriented motivations underlying conspiracy theories. *Group Processes & Intergroup Relations*, 27, 1050–1067. https://doi.org/10.1177/13684302241240696

Van Prooijen, J.-W., & Acker, M. (2015). The influence of control on belief in conspiracy theories: Conceptual and applied extensions. *Applied Cognitive Psychology*, 29, 753–761. https://doi.org/10.1002/acp.3161

Van Prooijen, J.-W., Amodio, D. M., Boot, A., Eerland, A., Etienne, T., Krouwel, A. P. M., Onderco, M., Verkoeijen, P., & Zwaan, R. A. (2023). A longitudinal analysis of conspiracy beliefs and Covid-19 health responses. *Psychological Medicine*, 53, 5709–5716. https://doi.org/10.1017/S0033291722002938

Van Prooijen, J.-W., & Böhm, N. (2023). Do conspiracy theories shape or rationalize vaccination hesitancy over time? *Social Psychological and Personality Science*, 15, 421–429. https://doi.org/10.1177/19485506231181659

Van Prooijen, J.-W., Cohen Rodrigues, T., Bunzel, C., Georgescu, O., Komáromy, D., & Krouwel, A. P. M. (2022). Populist gullibility: Conspiracy theories, news credibility, bullshit receptivity, and paranormal belief. *Political Psychology*, 43, 1061–1079. https://doi.org/10.1111/pops.12802

Van Prooijen, J.-W., Douglas, K., & De Inocencio, C. (2018). Connecting the dots: Illusory pattern perception predicts belief in conspiracies and the supernatural. *European Journal of Social Psychology*, 48, 320–335. https://doi.org/10.1002/ejsp.2331

Van Prooijen, J.-W., Etienne, T., Kutiyski, T., & Krouwel, A. P. M. (2023). Conspiracy beliefs prospectively predict health behavior and well-being during a pandemic. *Psychological Medicine*, 53, 2514–2521. https://doi.org/10.1017/S0033291721004438

Van Prooijen, J.-W., & Jostmann, N. B. (2013). Belief in conspiracy theories: The influence of uncertainty and perceived morality. *European Journal of Social Psychology*, 43, 109–115. https://doi.org/10.1002/ejsp.1922

Van Prooijen, J.-W., Kipperman, J., Li, Y., Mo, Y., & Nachtwey, P. (2025). Popcorn politics: Entertainment appraisals predict support for populist leaders. *British Journal of Psychology*. https://doi.org/10.1111/bjop.12791

Van Prooijen, J.-W., Krouwel, A. P. M., & Pollet, T. (2015). Political extremism predicts belief in conspiracy theories. *Social Psychological and Personality Science*, 6, 570–578. https://doi.org/10.1177/1948550614567356

Van Prooijen, J.-W., Ligthart, J., Rosema, S., & Xu, Y. (2022). The entertainment value of conspiracy theories. *British Journal of Psychology*, 113, 25–48. https://doi.org/10.1111/bjop.12522

Van Prooijen, J.-W., & Song, M. (2021). The cultural dimension of intergroup conspiracy theories. *British Journal of Psychology, 112,* 455–473. https://doi.org/10.1111/bjop.12471

Van Prooijen, J.-W. Šrol, J., & Maglić, M. (2025). How belief in conspiracy theories could harm sustainability. *Nature Human Behaviour.* https://doi.org/10.1038/s41562-025-02243-0

Van Prooijen, J.-W., Staman, J., & Krouwel, A. P. M. (2018). Increased conspiracy beliefs among ethnic and Muslim minorities. *Applied Cognitive Psychology, 32,* 661–667. https://doi.org/10.1002/acp.3442

Van Prooijen, J.-W., & Van Vugt, M. (2018). Conspiracy theories: Evolved functions and psychological mechanisms. *Perspectives on Psychological Science, 13,* 770–788. https://doi.org/10.1177/1745691618774270

Vosoughi, S., Roy, D., & Aral, S. (2018). The spread of true and false news online. *Science, 359,* 1146–1151. https://doi.org/10.1126/science.aap9559

Wang, H., & Van Prooijen, J.-W. (2023). Stolen elections: How conspiracy beliefs during the 2020 American presidential elections changed over time. *Applied Cognitive Psychology, 37,* 277–289. https://doi.org/10.1002/acp.3996

Whitson, J. A., Galinsky, A. D., & Kay, A. (2015). The emotional roots of conspiratorial perceptions, system justification, and belief in the paranormal. *Journal of Experimental Social Psychology, 56,* 89–95. https://doi.org/10.1016/j.jesp.2014.09.002

Wright, T. L., & Arbuthnot, J. (1974). Interpersonal trust, political preference, and perceptions of the Watergate affair. *Personality and Social Psychology Bulletin, 1,* 168–170. https://doi.org/10.1177/014616727400100158

Zhao, Q., Van Prooijen, J.-W., Jiang, X., & Spadaro, G. (2025). Suspicious of AI? Perceived autonomy and interdependence predict AI-related conspiracy beliefs. *British Journal of Social Psychology.* https://doi.org/10.1111/bjso.12883

Zhao, Q., Van Prooijen, J.-W., & Spadaro, G. (2024). Coping capacity attenuates the effect of natural disaster risk on conspiracy beliefs. *Journal of Environmental Psychology, 97,* 102363. https://doi.org/10.1016/j.jenvp.2024.102363